"This is a truly important book in the most urgent sense—a book that serves the cause of Christ by raising the most important question human beings face, and helping to answer it, no less. I am thankful to McKinley for his faithfulness and for the pastoral concern that prompted him to write such an important work."

> **R. Albert Mohler Jr.,** President, The Southern Baptist Theological Seminary

"Simple, piercing, winsome, practical, honest, direct, and pastoral. If you know *anyone* questioning their conversion (or who should be questioning!), get this book!"

> **Dave Harvey,** church care and church planting, Sovereign Grace Ministries; author, *Rescuing Ambition*

"Mike has always had the ability to talk about the mundane and serious aspects of life with both passion and depth in an endearing way. That is such a great and rare combination. Using those skills in his newest book, he references everyday experiences to explain much deeper and more important spiritual truths around the question of how do I know I am a Christian?"

> **Jackson Crum,** Lead Pastor, Park Community Church, Chicago, Illinois

"Really, is there anything more important to know about ourselves than whether we are actually Christians? People have come up with a lot of different ways of thinking about that question—ranging from your ability to remember 'praying the prayer,' to possessing a signed card in your Bible from a revival meeting, to ensuring your 'letter' is safely tucked away in some church's filing cabinet. Examining ourselves to make sure we are in the faith is about a whole lot more than that, and McKinley offers good help for that kind of heart evaluation. This is good devotional material, good small group material, and I expect that for some, it will probably even turn out to be the first time they've truly understood the gospel of Jesus Christ."

> **Greg Gilbert,** Senior Pastor, Third Avenue Baptist Church, Louisville, Kentucky

"There can be no more important question than 'Am I really a Christian?' and Mike McKinley helps us answer it with great skill. He manages to challenge nominal Christians while comforting genuine believers. McKinley's writing is accessible, engaging, and simple without ever being simplistic. I particularly appreciate the way he encourages us to explore this crucial question in the context of a Christian community. If you're not sure where you stand before God, or you know someone who's not sure, then this is the book for you."

Tim Chester, director, The Porterbrook Institute; author,
You Can Change and *A Meal with Jesus*

"Can any question in life be as important as knowing whether you are right with God—whether you are going to heaven or hell? I'm quite sure that every person now in eternity—with not a single exception among the billions there—would affirm the urgency and priority of pursuing the answer to such a question. That's why, if you have any uncertainties about the answer for your own situation, you should read this book. Some day, on a day as real as the one in which you entered the world, as real as the one in which you are reading these words, you will enter another world. There you will remain forever. Are you ready? If not, this book will help you understand how the Bible says to prepare."

Donald S. Whitney, Associate Professor of Biblical Spirituality, Senior Associate Dean of the School of Theology, The Southern Baptist Theological Seminary; author, *How Can I Be Sure I'm a Christian?*

Am I Really a Christian?

Mike McKinley

WHEATON, ILLINOIS

Am I Really a Christian?

Copyright 2011 by Mike McKinley

Published by Crossway
    1300 Crescent Street
    Wheaton, Illinois 60187

Cover design: Dual Identity inc.

Cover photo: Getty Images

First printing 2011

Printed in the United States of America

Trade paperback ISBN: 978-1-4335-2576-6
PDF ISBN: 978-1-4335-2577-3
Mobipocket ISBN: 978-1-4335-2578-0
EPub ISBN: 978-1-4335-2579-7

Library of Congress Cataloging-in-Publication Data
McKinley, Mike, 1975–
 Am I really a Christian? / Mike McKinley.
  p. cm.
 Includes index.
 ISBN 978-1-4335-2576-6 (tp)
  1. Theology, Doctrinal—Popular works. I. Title.
BT77.M1595   2011
230'.0462—dc22   2010053224

Crossway is a publishing ministry of Good News Publishers.

VP		25	24	23	22	21	20	19	18	17	16
16	15	14	13	12	11	10	9	8	7	6	

Am I Really a Christian?

Other 9Marks Books:

What Is the Gospel?
Greg Gilbert

Biblical Theology in the Life of the Church
Michael Lawrence

Church Planting Is for Wimps
Mike McKinley

It Is Well
Mark Dever and Michael Lawrence

What Does God Want of Us Anyway?
Mark Dever

The Church and the Surprising Offense of God's Love
Jonathan Leeman

What Is a Healthy Church Member?
Thabiti M. Anyabwile

12 Challenges Churches Face
Mark Dever

The Gospel and Personal Evangelism
Mark Dever

What Is a Healthy Church?
Mark Dever

The Message of the Old Testament: Promises Made
Mark Dever

The Deliberate Church: Building Your Ministry on the Gospel
Mark Dever

The Message of the New Testament: Promises Kept
Mark Dever

Nine Marks of a Healthy Church
Mark Dever

To four men
who have gone out of their way
to teach me what it means to be a Christian:

Darryle Owens
Jackson Crum
Mark Dever
and my dad

Contents

Foreword

Most of us think it is wise to visit a doctor every now and then for an examination. It is reassuring to gain a clean bill of health, but it is also a relief when we identify a problem before it is too late to deal with it. However, many of us who live in the world of "modern Christian America" (and beyond) recoil at the thought of examining our lives to see if God's Word gives our Christianity a clean bill of health. Yet this is precisely what Paul told the Corinthians when he said:

> Examine yourselves, to see whether you are in the faith. Test yourselves. Or do you not realize this about yourselves, that Jesus Christ is in you?—unless indeed you fail to meet the test! (2 Cor. 13:5)

The reality is that hell is heavily populated with people who professed Christianity but never examined themselves. It is too late if we venture into eternity only to hear these terrifying words from our Lord:

> "I never knew you; depart from me, you workers of lawlessness." (Matt. 7:23)

During my twenty years of walking with the Lord, I have longed to know that I am a true Christian and labored to understand the right relationship between faith and the fruit of good works. The problem is when we think that producing the right fruit will make us into the right kind of tree. The owner of any orchard will tell you that fruit is what a tree naturally produces and merely reveals the nature of that tree. If the fruit is gnarled, rotten, or nonexistent, hanging plastic fruit on the branches is not the solution.

"Doctor" Mike McKinley is just the guy to take us through this examination. Be assured that he has great bedside manner and cares deeply about our spiritual health—so much so that he invites all of us to look in the mirror of God's Word and ask the question: Am I really a Christian?

Kirk Cameron

Introduction:
Is This Book Mean Spirited?

Well, here we are, at the introduction. Congratulations to you on successfully navigating the table of contents and Library of Congress information and making it this far! At this point, it is customary to do some introducing, specifically of myself and this book. So let's start there.

This is a book aimed at convincing you that you may not be a Christian. I want you to ask the question, "Am I really a Christian?" because I'm convinced there are a lot of people in this world who think they are Christians but are not.

Hearing that, you might be tempted to ask, "What kind of self-important jerk writes a book like this? Who delights in insulting and disillusioning people?" And, to be honest, I am a self-important jerk much of the time. You can ask my friends.

But if you will believe it, I am writing this book because I genuinely want to help. We who profess to be Christians in the world today have a serious problem. Many of us are confused about a matter that is larger than life and death, namely, whether everyone who claims to be a Christian really is.

Let me explain. A lot of subcultures and cliques are notoriously picky about who really "belongs." When I was younger, I used to hang out with punk rockers. In those circles we had endless debates about whether some person or some band was a "real" punk. If you didn't meet the right criteria or espouse a pure ideology, you were labeled a fake, a phony, a wannabe. In the world of punk rock orthodoxy, the worst thing that could happen to you was being branded a poseur. But who finally cares about the boundaries of punk rock, right? No one's eternal destiny depends on whether the punk bona fides are in order or not.

Here's another example. Spend a few days with me and you'll discover I am a huge New York Yankees fan. I travel with my family to watch the team play; I watch most of their games on the television; I name my pets after the Yankees players; I am in a bad mood when the Yankees lose (which, fortunately, is not all that often).

Now let's say that you claim to be a huge Yankees fan as well. Yet as we talk, it becomes clear that you have not been to a game in years. You don't really know who is on the roster. You just check in around play-off time and ride the wave to World Series glory. Well, you would not qualify as a "huge Yankees fan" in my book. I would consider you a casual fan and something of a front-runner.

But again, who really cares? People don't live or die because they are not huge Yankees fans. In the final accounting, it is pretty meaningless. However, turn the topic to whether you are a Christian, and suddenly we have left the realm of the trivial and we are swimming in the deep end. Nothing less than the eternal fate of your soul is at stake.

Jesus taught that the world was divided into two groups of people who would experience two radically different fates in this life and in the next. Those who are his followers will receive abundant life now and eternal blessings in his presence (John 10:10; Matt. 25:34). Those who are not his followers will squander their time on earth and ultimately experience the just wrath of God against their sins for all eternity. Friend, you have a lot at stake in knowing whether you are genuinely a Christian.

Imagine for a minute that we're all running in a race. According to the rules of this race, it doesn't matter how we place, but it is absolutely critical that we finish. Not only that, our eternal destiny hangs on whether we finish this race. Finishing means eternal joy. Failing to finish, for whatever reason, means eternal suffering. This would be a pretty important race, would it not?

Now imagine that, looking along the racecourse, we see people dressed in running shorts and fancy sneakers, but for some reason they are sitting by the side of the road. Other people are crouched down, still as statues, tense, poised, and ready in the starting blocks. But they never move; they just stay there. Some people are wandering around in circles. Still others are running the wrong way.

Suppose then we stop to talk to these wayward runners and non-runners. Quickly it becomes clear that they are convinced they're running well. They say they're looking forward to completing the race and receiving the substantial reward. They smile and talk dreamily about life beyond the finish line. The problem is, we know that they will never finish the race given their pace or direction.

Tell me: What would be the loving thing to do in that case? Would love motivate us to ignore their confusion? Would love motivate us to politely nod and say nothing? Of course not. Love would require us to warn them, to convince them, to plead with them to change their course.

That is the spirit in which I offer this book to you. I hope to serve you by helping you determine if you are "running your race" in the right direction.

With that in mind, here are four points of clarification. First, I don't think that I'm any better than you. I stand in the same place as you. I need to examine my life just as I'm asking you to examine yours.

Second, this book is intended for people who claim to be Christians or want to be Christians. If you know you are not a Christian (say, because you are a Muslim or an agnostic or anything else) you are welcome to keep reading, but you may find that other books will do a better job of speaking to your questions and issues.

Third, I don't think that I'm an expert in these matters. You shouldn't believe anything just because I say it. After all, I can barely balance my checkbook. Instead, my goal is to show you what the experts have said. I want to go to the Bible and see what Jesus and the authors of Scripture have said on the matter. I assume that because you think of yourself as a Christian, you are willing to do and believe and respond to whatever God's Word says.

Fourth, I realize that a lot of people who are genuine Christians struggle with assurance. As a pastor, I often meet with brothers and sisters with sensitive consciences who feel every failure and struggle acutely. If that describes you, then you may want to enlist the help of some friends as you read through this book. Ask them not only to challenge you, but also to encourage you with God's grace in your life. Or failing that, just skip ahead to chapter 8, which is described below.

Here is where we are going: In the first chapter, I want to look more closely at what Jesus and the apostle Paul said about the gravity of this matter. We'll see that simply saying that you are a Christian doesn't mean you really are one. In the second chapter, we will look at what the Bible says about what constitutes a "genuine" Christian.

In chapters 3 through 7, we will look at passages in the Bible that give us some specific criteria for determining that we are not genuine Christians. In chapter 8, we will consider the matter of assurance. After spending so much time on criteria for determining if you are not a Christian, which is really the main purpose of this book, it does seem important to also spend a few moments considering how to know if you really *are* a Christian.

In chapter 9, we will conclude by looking at the role of the local church in helping you know whether you are a Christian. In fact, as you read through this book, I hope you do it together with members of your church. God has given us local churches so that we have brothers and sisters in Christ who know us well and can help us answer this most important question.

Becoming a Christian means admitting that you are a sinner, and admitting that you are sinner means admitting that you are prone to self-deceit. Gratefully, God has given us other Christians to help us see the things we cannot see about ourselves. Therefore, you might say that this isn't a book for individual Christians. It is a book for Christians in churches. The Christian who thinks he can do the sort of self-examination we're going to do in this book *apart* from other members in his or her local church is off to a bad start and may never find the answers he or she is looking for.

Well, that seems like enough of an introduction. I'm glad you have stuck around. Now let's hear what Jesus says on the issue at hand.

1

You Are Not a Christian
Just Because You Say That You Are

MY E-MAIL IN-BOX is clogged with opportunities to "become something." Just this month, I have received messages from friends and spambots both offering me the chance to become:

- someone's friend on Facebook,
- a member of Netflix,
- a member of the Democratic Party,
- part of a fantasy football league,
- an ESPN.com "insider,"
- part of an organization's board of trustees,
- the recipient of an ATM card from the Central Bank of Nigeria (preprogramed with $10 million on it!).

I probably will not take advantage of any of these opportunities. I am already an ESPN.com "insider," and I don't have time to play fantasy football or be a trustee (though come to think of it, maybe I should follow up on the $10 million).

Still, consider what would happen if I were to avail myself of these kinds of offers: my relationship with those groups would become redefined, and I would clearly be a member. Not a lot of ambiguity here. Such group membership is a matter of self-selection: you either opt "in" or you opt "out." Right now, both Netflix and I have a good grasp on the status of our relationship (or nonrelationship) because I have never opted in. But here's the kicker: being a Christian is not exactly like that.

God Knows His Own

To be sure, there is great clarity on God's side of the equation. He is not confused about who does and does not belong to him. In the Bible, we read that God has a definite record of those who will receive eternal life through Christ. When the seventy-two disciples return to Jesus, giddy from their recent ministry success, Jesus tells them, "Do not rejoice in this, that the spirits are subject to you, but rejoice that *your names are written in heaven*" (Luke 10:20). Elsewhere, Jesus tells the disciples, "I am the good shepherd. *I know my own* and my own know me" (John 10:14). God knows who is truly a Christian and who is not.

That's why the apostle Paul can speak of "Clement and the rest of my fellow workers, whose names are *in the book of life*" (Phil. 4:3). So, too, the apostle John, in his vision of the final judgment before the great white throne, refers to a "book of life" which contains all the names of those who are truly God's people. Everyone whose name is *not* listed in this book will be thrown into the lake of fire, while everyone whose name does appear will gain entrance into the New Jerusalem (Rev. 20:15; 21:27). So God knows who belongs to him and who doesn't. He's not short on clarity.

Your Spiritual Shirt Is Inside Out

However, the same cannot be said about us. We don't see ourselves that clearly. In fact, our self-awareness is often comically limited.

Have you ever realized that you have been walking around with toilet paper stuck to your shoe? Or with your shirt on backward? Or with a blob of ketchup on your cheek? I've done each of these at one time or another. When someone finally had mercy on me and pointed out the problem ("Hey, moron, your shirt is on backward!") I felt a small-to-moderate sense of embarrassment. I had been walking around assuming certain things about myself (suave, devastatingly handsome, capable of dressing myself properly), but in that moment I discovered that reality was otherwise (not cool at all). Everyone around me could see the truth about me clearly, but I was oblivious.

I remember one occasion in particular that God used to teach me about the sometimes gaping difference between self-perception and reality. I had just become an assistant pastor. I had had the opportunity to lead a Bible study of about two hundred people in our church. I enjoyed leading the discussion and answering questions. By all accounts the Bible study seemed to go pretty well.

The next day I was sitting in the office of a friend of mine named Matt, and I asked him to give me some feedback about the study from the previous night. He told me that he, too, thought that it had gone well, and then he mentioned how surprised he was by the way I led the group. "Mike," he said, "I could not believe how warm and friendly and connected you seemed. You really looked like you were glad to be there and engaged with people well. I was surprised."

Matt meant these words as a compliment, but I didn't take them that way. I pushed back: What did he mean that he was surprised? I am always warm and friendly and engaged! I always look like I am glad to be there! I prided myself on engaging people well. After all, I've always known that I wasn't going to get ahead in life based on overwhelming intelligence; people with my limited wattage need to be warm and friendly.

But Matt didn't see me like this. He explained that, though he liked me personally, he had always perceived me as aloof and a little distant. To make matters worse, he began to give me some very specific examples of times that he had observed me behaving that way.

As you can imagine, I was disturbed by Matt's words. After I left his office, I turned his words over and over in my mind. Finally, I came to the conclusion that he was crazy. Or if he was not crazy, at least he was overly critical. Even though Matt was a trusted friend who had known me for ten years, I was convinced that my perception of myself was right and his perception was wrong.

That afternoon I had a lunch appointment with Steve, who was another member of the church. I didn't know Steve very well at the time, but in the course of his involvement with the church he had had plenty of opportunities to observe me in action. While we ate, I relayed to Steve the details of my earlier conversation with Matt. When I finished, I asked him if he agreed. I wasn't really an aloof and distant person, was I?

Much to my surprise, Steve nodded his head furiously. Through a mouthful of enchiladas he said, "Yup. That's absolutely you. You're totally that way. Aloof . . . I like that. That's a good word for it." He then shared in detail why he thought I was. By the time my lunch with Steve was over, I was convinced that he and Matt were right about me.

I was also devastated. My perception of myself had been laughably inaccurate. I had been sure that I was Mr. Friendly, but everyone else thought that I was Mr. Distant-and-Intimidating. How could I have been so completely blind to the truth about myself? Have you ever felt that way?

The Only Opinion That Matters

In Matthew 25, Jesus tells us about a group of people who come to realize the truth about themselves only after it is too late. He sets the scene for a harrowing account of what the final judgment will be like:

> When the Son of Man comes in his glory, and all the angels
> with him, then he will sit on his glorious throne. Before him
> will be gathered all the nations, and he will separate people one
> from another as a shepherd separates the sheep from the goats.
> (Matt. 25:31–32)

The sheep here represent God's people, the true followers of Christ. They are praised by their master and ushered into "the kingdom prepared for you from the foundation of the world" (Matt. 25:34). Theirs is the fate that we want!

The goats, on the other hand, do not fare well at all. Listen to what Jesus says to them:

> Then he will say to those on his left, "Depart from me, you
> cursed, into the eternal fire prepared for the devil and his an-
> gels. For I was hungry and you gave me no food, I was thirsty
> and you gave me no drink, I was a stranger and you did not wel-
> come me, naked and you did not clothe me, sick and in prison
> and you did not visit me." Then they also will answer, saying,
> "Lord, when did we see you hungry or thirsty or a stranger or
> naked or sick or in prison, and did not minister to you?" Then
> he will answer them, saying, "Truly, I say to you, as you did not
> do it to one of the least of these, you did not do it to me." And
> these will go away into eternal punishment, but the righteous
> into eternal life. (Matt. 25:41–46)

There are many things that we could say about this passage, which is why we'll return to it in chapter 6. But two things are important for us to see right now. First, everyone gathered before that throne either considered themselves to be Christians or at least expected Christ's approval. When Jesus confronted the goats with their eternal destruction, no one threw up their hands and said, "You are right Jesus! I was wrong. I always said that you did not really exist. I never believed in you. I should never have decided to reject you after all!"

None of them were consciously opposed to Jesus. In fact, when they heard Jesus's verdict, they seemed to think that there must have been some mistake. They all showed up for the big event expecting to receive a reward from Jesus. But they were terribly wrong. They were self-deceived. They did not see their own state clearly, and their blindness cost them everything.

Second, notice that Jesus himself is the judge. He is the one who ushers people into eternal life or eternal punishment. The nations gathered before him do not make that decision. There is nothing they can say or do to change his mind. The only thing that matters on that last day is whether Jesus says that you are one of his.

When you stand before Jesus your judge, any evidence you marshal on your own behalf won't matter. You might point to all the times you prayed "The Sinner's Prayer," or the time you walked down the aisle, or your baptism, or the other time you were baptized in case the first one didn't "take," or the youth retreats you attended, or the missions trips you went on. But if, in that final moment, Jesus does not look at you and say, "She is one of my sheep" or "He belongs to me," none of that will matter. You will not be able to argue with the Judge's verdict. Jesus himself said in the Sermon on the Mount:

> Not everyone who says to me, "Lord, Lord," will enter the king-
> dom of heaven, but the one who does the will of my Father who
> is in heaven. On that day many will say to me, "Lord, Lord, did
> we not prophesy in your name, and cast out demons in your
> name, and do many mighty works in your name?" And then
> will I declare to them, "I never knew you; depart from me, you
> workers of lawlessness." (Matt. 7:21–23)

Can you see what Jesus is saying? It is possible for you to honestly believe that you are a follower of Christ, but not actually be one. It is possible to say to him, "Lord, Lord," but never enter the kingdom of heaven. Merely checking a box and calling yourself a Christian doesn't mean that you really are a Christian.

Recently, a high-profile website was established where people can sign their names and publicly "declare their faith in the Lord Jesus Christ." I suppose that's fine if that's your cup of tea. But God will not refer to such a website on the day of judgment. It is his evaluation of you that ultimately matters, not yours. As Jesus said, only those who do the will of the Father in heaven are really Christians. Everyone else will hear Jesus say, "Depart from me."

An Unpleasant Surprise

I realize that what I'm saying is different from what many churches teach these days. In their well-intentioned desire to make the good news of Jesus available to everyone, many churches make the decision to follow Jesus a little too easy. They make it about the *decision*. Just *say* you want to be a Christian, and you are one. Pray these words. Sign this card. Follow those steps. Presto, you are a Christian. End of story. Case closed. Welcome to heaven!

It is true that we need to make a onetime decision to follow Jesus. But a true onetime decision is followed by the everyday decision to *follow* Jesus. Jesus did not think that it was enough just to superficially identify yourself with him. There is more to being his follower than just a profession of faith. My fear is that too many churches have encouraged people to expect that Jesus will one day say to them, "Well done, faithful servant." But in fact, they will hear him say, "Depart from me." Such people will discover the truth only after it is too late.

Is it possible that you could be one of those people? Could it be that you are not really a Christian? How can you be sure?

Jesus Isn't Willy Wonka

Admittedly, this is a complicated subject, and there are lots of ways our thinking can go wrong. One misunderstanding we must guard against concerns the character of Jesus.

Do you remember the classic 1971 film *Willy Wonka & the Chocolate Factory*? (I'm talking about the old freaky one starring Gene Wilder, not the new freaky one starring Johnny Depp.) After our heroes Charlie and Grandpa Joe have survived an arduous tour of the Wonka Chocolate Factory, they go to collect the grand prize that's been promised to them: a lifetime supply of Wonka chocolate. But there's a surprise at the end. Willy Wonka, the factory owner, denies Charlie the prize based on a technicality. The scene goes like this:

GRANDPA JOE: Mr. Wonka?

WILLY WONKA: I am extraordinarily busy, sir.

GRANDPA JOE: I just wanted to ask about the chocolate. Uh, the lifetime supply of chocolate . . . for Charlie. When does he get it?

WILLY WONKA: He doesn't.

GRANDPA JOE: Why not?

WILLY WONKA: Because he broke the rules.

GRANDPA JOE: What rules? We didn't see any rules, did we, Charlie?

WILLY WONKA: Wrong, sir! Wrong! Under section 37B of the contract signed by him, it states quite clearly that all offers shall become null and void if—and you can read it for yourself in this photostatic copy: I, the undersigned, shall forfeit all rights, privileges, and licenses herein and herein contained, et cetera, et cetera . . . Fax mentis incendium gloria cultum, et cetera, et cetera . . . Memo bis punitor delicatum! It is all there, black and white, clear as crystal! You stole fizzy lifting drinks! You bumped into the ceiling which now has to be washed and sterilized, so you get nothing! You lose! Good day, sir!

GRANDPA JOE: You're a crook. You're a cheat and a swindler! That's what you are! How could you do something like this, build up a little boy's hopes and then smash all his dreams to pieces? You're an inhuman monster!
WILLY WONKA: I said, "Good day!"[1]

Here is the misunderstanding to guard against: Jesus is not like Willy Wonka. Our God is not a God who delights in keeping people in the dark, only to pull the rug out from under them in the last minute and deny them the rewards he promised. He is not a miser looking to withhold blessings on a technicality.

Instead, God delights in saving his people. Jesus says that he "came to seek and to save the lost" (Luke 19:10). That is why he came to earth, to save us from our sins. If he didn't want to save us, he would not have come in the first place. Jesus is not a cheat. He is not a swindler. He is not an inhumane monster. Nothing could be further from the truth.

Furthermore, Jesus has graciously given us extremely clear guidance about who truly belongs to him. In the verses leading up to the passage we read a moment ago, in which Jesus says he will tell some to depart, he explains, "You will recognize them by their fruits" (Matt. 7:20). In the verses following this same passage, Jesus gives an illustration of a man who hears Jesus's words and "does them" being like a wise man who builds on solid rock. Meanwhile, the man who hears Jesus's words but "does not do them" is like a foolish man who builds on sand (Matt. 7:24–27). There are no hidden clauses here. Jesus is looking, quite simply, for "the one who does the will of my Father who is in heaven" (Matt. 7:21).

Examine Yourself!

The very fact that Jesus tells us about the danger we are in is proof of his love and mercy. He has given us these warnings and he wants us to heed them. His words should ring in our souls like a fire alarm. His cautions are meant to help us reach that last day without being self-deceived.

For the same reasons, the apostle Paul instructs the church in Corinth, "Examine yourselves, to see whether you are in the faith. Test yourselves" (2 Cor. 13:5). Likewise, the apostle Peter instructs, "Be all the more diligent to make your calling and election sure, for if you practice these qualities you will never fall. For in this way there will be richly provided for you an entrance into the eternal kingdom of our Lord and Savior Jesus Christ" (2 Pet. 1:10–11). Paul and Peter loved the people who would read their letters, and so they warned them to look carefully at their lives before it was too late.

That is what I hope to do throughout this book. I want to look at some of the places in Scripture where Jesus tells us exactly on what basis we can *examine ourselves* to see whether we are in the faith. Ideally, this should be done in the context of a local church. Because we are not always the best judges of our own lives and behavior, it is extremely important to have wise and honest Christians around us who can help us see things in our lives that we cannot see on our own. So find someone in your church (or, maybe find a church!) to ask to come along with you on this journey. But first, we have one more bit of legwork to do.

How to Respond

Reflect:

Does Jesus's warning in Matthew 7:21–23 make you uncomfortable? Why?

Why do you think it is not enough to just say that you are a Christian?

Have you ever examined your life to see whether you are really a Christian? If not, why not? If so, what criteria did you use? What did you conclude?

Repent:

> Ask God to forgive you for any ways that you have been wrongly confident about your spiritual state.

> Think of one way you could grow in humility and learn to not always trust your own perception of things.

Remember:

> Think about 2 Corinthians 5:21: "For our sake he made him to be sin who knew no sin, so that in him we might become the righteousness of God."

> You will never be righteous enough to please God. But thankfully, Christ's perfect righteousness becomes ours when we come to him in faith. Praise God for that good news!

Report:

> Talk to a leader or friend in your church and ask for honest, regular feedback about your spiritual life.

2

You Are Not a Christian
If You Haven't Been Born Again

IF I AM GOING TO TRY to convince you that you may not
be a Christian, it seems as if we need to define what the word
Christian means. Literally the word *Christian* means "a follower
of Christ." According to Acts 11, the label was first used in the
city of Antioch in the first century to describe the men and
women who had joined the small group of followers of Jesus. It
was probably meant as a term of derision, but members of the
early church came to embrace it and use it to describe themselves. The apostle Peter used the word Christian in his first letter to indicate that his readers were true followers of the Lord.
He writes there, "Yet if anyone suffers as a Christian, let him not
be ashamed, but let him glorify God in that name" (1 Pet. 4:16).

Unpacking it a bit more, a Christian is someone who
has heard the gospel word, the good news about Jesus, and
responded by trusting in Jesus for salvation and declaring him
as Lord. In short, a Christian believes:

1. We are sinners, fully deserving the condemnation of a holy
   God who hates all sin and wickedness.
2. God, in his mercy, took on human flesh in the person of
   Jesus and lived the perfect life of obedience to God that we
   should have lived.

3. He gave up his life, on the cross, to bear the penalty for our sins, and he was raised from the dead in victory and glory as God's promised King.
4. Anyone who turns to Jesus in repentance and faith is completely forgiven and adopted into God's family.

Sadly, however, it seems as if the term *Christian* was drained of meaning even before the ink on Peter's letter was dry. Throughout the New Testament Epistles, the apostles spend a surprising amount of time warning against false teachers and straying church members, many of whom, no doubt, were continuing to call themselves Christians.

Nowadays we use the term as an adjective to describe all kinds of things that have little to do with following Christ. One online retailer advertises "Christian car accessories," "Christian tote bags," and "Christian afghans." The connection between Peter's use of Christian and rubber car mats is not immediately clear to me. But business is business!

We are also promiscuous with our use of the term as a noun. We use it as a default category to indicate that someone is not a Jew or a Muslim. Or, we use it to embrace famous people who were raised in a church culture such as squeaky-clean, virginal pop stars just because they cut their teeth singing in churches. (Think Britney Spears, then Jessica Simpson, then Clay Aiken.) Then, when their shorts become too short and their lives become intolerably scandalous, we begin to have our doubts. Maybe they weren't really Christians to begin with. Maybe they were just from the southern United States. Sometimes it can be hard to tell the difference. So what does it mean to be a Christian?

A Working Definition

We could slice this apple in a number of ways. But for our purposes, I want to suggest this working definition: *a Christian is someone who has received the new birth as a free gift from God.*

Certainly we could say more. We could frame our definition by using different theological categories like adoption ("a Christian is someone who is a child of God") or justification ("a Christian is someone who has received right standing before God"). But I want to approach this subject through the lens of regeneration, which is why I will talk about being "born again" or receiving "the new birth," two phrases I will use interchangeably. With this chapter, I will unpack this definition and clarify a few things about being a Christian with five questions.

What Is the New Birth?

Jesus first speaks of the new birth in the third chapter of John's Gospel. That's the best place for us to begin:

> Now there was a man of the Pharisees named Nicodemus, a ruler of the Jews. This man came to Jesus by night and said to him, "Rabbi, we know that you are a teacher come from God, for no one can do these signs that you do unless God is with him." Jesus answered him, "Truly, truly, I say to you, unless one is born again he cannot see the kingdom of God." Nicodemus said to him, "How can a man be born when he is old? Can he enter a second time into his mother's womb and be born?" Jesus answered, "Truly, truly, I say to you, unless one is born of water and the Spirit, he cannot enter the kingdom of God. That which is born of the flesh is flesh, and that which is born of the Spirit is spirit. Do not marvel that I said to you, 'You must be born again.' The wind blows where it wishes, and you hear its sound, but you do not know where it comes from or where it goes. So it is with everyone who is born of the Spirit." (John 3:1–8)

Surely, this was not the conversation Nicodemus expected to have with Jesus. He knew something was different about Jesus and that Jesus seemed to have the key to the promised coming of God's kingdom. But he was not expecting this! After all,

Nicodemus was a teacher of Israel. He may not have been as popular as Jesus, but he did have a seat among the religious elite. He came to Jesus looking for the missing piece, the thing that he needed to get over the top.

But Jesus's prescription sounded like advice to remodel a kitchen with dynamite. This was no Dr. Phil–style "5 Tips to a Better You!" No, Jesus told Nicodemus to completely start over—to be born again! Even though he was a model of religious rigor and devotion, Nicodemus needed a totally new life, a new birth.

You can imagine Nicodemus's confusion. He was probably a little nervous about coming to Jesus. Jesus had been turning water into wine, overturning tables in the temple, and saying things like "Destroy this temple, and in three days I will raise it up" (John 2:19). Jesus wasn't afraid to say things that didn't make sense to the majority of people around him. But now he tells Nicodemus that to enter God's kingdom he must get birthed all over again.

The poor man clearly didn't understand. Carefully he pressed Jesus for more details: "Umm, Jesus? You know that's impossible, right? Old people are not born a second time. It is kind of a onetime thing."

So Jesus clarified what he meant. He wasn't talking about physical renewal, but about being "born of the Spirit." Nicodemus needed a totally new spiritual life. He needed what theologians call "regeneration," a rebirth whereby the old spiritual person gives way to a new spiritual person.

If Nicodemus needed to be born again, even in the days when Jesus was walking around, then you and I today surely need to be born again in order to see the kingdom that Jesus brought. Remember our working definition of a Christian: a Christian is someone who has received the new birth as a free gift from God. This is what separates the Christian from the rest of the world; the Christian has received new spiritual life from God.

Why Is the New Birth Necessary?

Although Jesus was perfectly clear with Nicodemus about his need for regeneration, he didn't tell Nicodemus why he needed this new life, which may seem strange. The suggestion that a respected religious leader would need such a radical spiritual overhaul surely would have been scandalous. Why was a new birth necessary?

Jesus did, in fact, give Nicodemus a clue. Nicodemus had asked how these things could be, to which Jesus replied, "Are you the teacher of Israel and yet you do not understand these things?" (John 3:10). Jesus thought that Nicodemus had enough information from the Old Testament Scriptures to be able to understand what he was saying. The Old Testament, which Nicodemus would have known inside and out, was full of indications that such a radical transformation was both needed and promised by God.

There are two things that Nicodemus should have realized. First, the Old Testament speaks of all humans as living in dire spiritual straits. Some examples:

- King David indicts the enemies of God: "For there is no truth in their mouth; their inmost self is destruction; their throat is an open grave; they flatter with their tongue" (Ps. 5:9).
- But it is not just a certain set of people who are God's enemies. Every human being who has ever lived has been an enemy of God. David writes about the human condition: "The LORD looks down from heaven on the children of man, to see if there are any who understand, who seek after God. They have all turned aside; together they have become corrupt; there is none who does good, not even one" (Ps. 14:2–3).
- God even says that his chosen people, Israel, have hearts of stone (Ezek. 36:26). Stone hearts don't work very well. A person with a stone heart is dead, unfeeling, and unaware.

When you put it all together, the picture is bleak, hopeless even. Human beings are not spiritually wounded; we are spiritually dead. It is not just that we are unwilling to please God; we are unable to please him. Nicodemus would not have read the apostle Paul, of course. But so that this point is clear to us, it is worth noticing that Paul picked up on this Old Testament theme of our dire spiritual condition:

- He writes in one place, "For the mind that is set on the flesh is hostile to God, for it does not submit to God's law; indeed, it cannot. Those who are in the flesh cannot please God" (Rom. 8:7–8).
- And in another, "You were dead in the trespasses and sins in which you once walked, following the course of this world, following the prince of the power of the air, the spirit that is now at work in the sons of disobedience—among whom we all once lived in the passions of our flesh, carrying out the desires of the body and the mind, and were by nature children of wrath, like the rest of mankind" (Eph. 2:1–3).

Self-improvement is not the solution to these kinds of problems. A radical overhaul is.

I learned a little something about the difference between these two kinds of solutions when I purchased my present home. My wife and I bought our house at the height of the real estate boom in northern Virginia. The neighborhood was strategic for ministry purposes, and it had plenty of space for family and friends. We could even afford it—almost—which was unheard of at the time. Indeed, it was a perfect house . . . except for the small fact that it looked like it belonged on the set of a really violent horror movie.

Over the next couple of years I undertook the work of cleaning up the house. Dead animals were removed from the backyard. Some walls were torn down. Others were scrubbed with TSP to remove the decades of nicotine buildup. Random doors were walled up and floors were replaced. But throughout this time, I knew that I would eventually have to deal with the master bedroom's walk-in closet.

You see, the gutters above this little room had been clogged for decades, and over time the siding, insulation, and drywall had become comprised of rot. One morning, our dog Jeter was bored in the yard and dug a hole through the wall. My wife went to the closet to get dressed, only to see the dog peering in at her from the outside.

At this point, of course, I had to bite the bullet and do something. A friend came to help me, and over the course of many summer weekends we rebuilt the closet. Every stud had to come out; they were all decayed. Every piece of drywall had to go; they were all disintegrating and moldy. Every scrap of insulation went to the dump, along with the siding and trim. By the time we were done, the closet was completely rebuilt. Nothing remained from the original closet because nothing in the original closet would have been at all useful in a nice, noninfectious house.

That closet presents a dim picture of our spiritual condition. We are not damaged by sin; we are utterly destroyed by it. We are not like a board that has come loose and needs a couple of nails. We are like a closet that is so badly rotten that every scrap needs to be replaced. Nicodemus should have read the story of Israel in the Old Testament and known this.

Second, Nicodemus should have known from the Old Testament that God had promised to fix this terrible problem. God doesn't just point out our wretched condition and leave us there. He promises to intervene and save us. As he said through Ezekiel, "I will give you a new heart, and a new spirit I will put within you. And I will remove the heart of stone from your flesh and give you a heart of flesh. And I will put my Spirit within you, and cause you to walk in my statutes and be careful to obey my rules" (Ezek. 36:26–27). God himself would make his people alive by giving them his Spirit.

So when Jesus entered the scene and told Nicodemus that he needed a completely new life wrought by the Spirit of God, his reaction should have been, "This is what we have been waiting for all this time! This is what we need!"

How Do You Get the New Birth?

But this isn't what Nicodemus was thinking. He was looking for a spiritual tune-up, a buff-and-polish job. But Jesus prescribed nothing less than radical heart surgery, which led to Nicodemus's utter confusion. Notice, Jesus even had to tell him "do not marvel," as if he had to reach over and close Nicodemus's gaping mouth.

You can probably sympathize with his perplexity. Nicodemus knew that he could not be "born again" all by himself. Sure enough, Jesus observed that this was the work of God's Spirit and that God's Spirit acted entirely according to his own pleasure, like the wind blowing wherever it wishes. So what was Nicodemus supposed to do? How could he get the new spiritual birth that he so desperately needed?

The bad news, which Nicodemus saw clearly, is that people cannot give themselves this new birth. It is completely impossible. But the good news, which Jesus spent a lot of time explaining throughout his ministry, was that he had come to make this extremely impossible thing possible.

Through his life, death, and resurrection, Jesus secured new life for his people. God in his mercy applies that work of Jesus to our lives, giving us new life through his Spirit. In 1 Peter 1:3–4, the apostle reflects on what God has done for us:

> Blessed be the God and Father of our Lord Jesus Christ! According to his great mercy, he has caused us to be born again to a living hope through the resurrection of Jesus Christ from the dead, to an inheritance that is imperishable, undefiled, and unfading, kept in heaven for you.

Regeneration is a unilateral act of God. God does the merciful work. God makes us alive. We simply receive his gift.

What Is the Result of Being Born Again?

When God does his marvelous work of regeneration in a spiritually dead person, it always produces results. In Acts 16:14, we read of the work of God in the life of a woman named Lydia. Luke writes, "One who heard us was a woman named Lydia, from the city of Thyatira, a seller of purple goods, who was a worshiper of God. The Lord opened her heart to pay attention to what was said by Paul." The Lord acted on Lydia's heart, and Lydia gave heed to Paul's preaching of the gospel and responded to it with faith. That's how the new birth works.

The Bible calls that result "conversion." God's gift of the new birth always has an effect on our lives. It changes us; it converts us from one way of life to another. The Spirit of God does not make us alive and then leave us alone; he gives us new faith, new loves, and new desires. The new life that we have by God's Spirit causes a change in us. It makes us turn from our love of sin and turn to Christ in trust and faith. So he acts, and then we act.

This is radical stuff. It is not like switching your brand of deodorant; it is a total alteration of your spiritual state. It is a change of cosmic allegiances. Paul puts it this way: "If anyone is in Christ, he is a new creation. The old has passed away; behold, the new has come. All this is from God, who through Christ reconciled us to himself" (2 Cor. 5:17–18). If you are in Christ, if you have been born again, you are a totally new creature.

Now, we need to be careful once more about guarding against misunderstandings. While the internal change in our natures may be radical and immediate, the changes in some of our external attitudes and behaviors may manifest themselves more slowly. Regeneration does not immediately take away all indwelling sin. The Bible is realistic. The apostle Paul, whose conversion was sudden and dramatic, even admitted to struggling with sin throughout his life (e.g., Rom. 7:15).

But wherever the Spirit of God has given new life, there will always be transformation, even though the change may be slow at times. That is the key point that you must understand. The transition from the kingdom of darkness into God's marvelous light (1 Pet. 2:9) will make a difference in a person's life.

For instance, Paul lists some of the visible fruit that the Spirit of God will produce in the believer's emotions, conduct, and attitudes: "The fruit of the Spirit is love, joy, peace, patience, kindness, goodness, faithfulness, gentleness, self-control; against such things there is no law. And those who belong to Christ Jesus have crucified the flesh with its passions and desires" (Gal. 5:22–24). Such fruit is the result of the Spirit's gracious work in our souls.

How Can You Tell That You Are Born Again?

Here finally is the big question—how can you tell that you've been born again? Regeneration, after all, isn't usually flashy. It doesn't wear neon signs. It doesn't create a halo over your head. It doesn't give you superpowers or remarkable capacities for solving complex trigonometry problems. In other words, it is not always easy to tell who has received the gift of regeneration.

But that does not mean that there is no way to examine yourself to see whether you are really born again. Instead, you should look for the fruit. Alarm bells may not go off at the moment of regeneration, but it always results in a changed life. It is an invisible act of God that can only be seen in the changed attitudes and passions and desires of the Christian. The Spirit always bears fruit in the lives of people he makes alive.

Again, I can't stress enough that this important process

of examination can only be properly done in the context of a faithful local church. You need other Christians who are committed to your spiritual well-being. They are the ones who will be able to get to know you and identify the fruit of the new birth in your life. If you are prone to discouragement and self-condemnation, they may be able to encourage you. If you are (like me!) prone to an inflated view of yourself, they may be able to let a little air out of your bubble for your own good.

Five Things All Christians Have

What constitutes reliable evidence of regeneration? In the upcoming chapters I want to look at five things that the Bible says will always accompany true conversion. If you have these things, you have firm evidence of God's regenerating work in your life. If these things are absent, you have reason to be concerned.

> *Belief in true doctrine.* You're not a Christian just because you like Jesus.
> *Hatred for sin in your life.* You're not a Christian if you enjoy sin.
> *Perseverance over time.* You're not a Christian if you don't persist in the faith.
> *Love for other people.* You're not a Christian if you don't have care and concern for other people.
> *Freedom from love of the world.* You're not a Christian if the things of the world are more valuable to you than God.

God has commanded us to examine ourselves to see whether we are in the faith. These five things make up some of the criteria by which we can judge ourselves. For the professing Christian, then, the all-important question is: Do I have the fruit of the new birth in my life?

On the last day, nothing else will matter. If you have not

been born again, you will not enter the kingdom of God. It will not matter that you have Christian parents or that you grew up in a church. As John the Baptist told the Pharisees,

> Bear fruit in keeping with repentance. And do not presume to say to yourselves, "We have Abraham as our father," for I tell you, God is able from these stones to raise up children for Abraham. Even now the axe is laid to the root of the trees. Every tree therefore that does not bear good fruit is cut down and thrown into the fire. (Matt. 3:8–10)

We don't want to be presumptuous like the Pharisees. Therefore, we need to continually examine the fruit in our lives. We should do this by ourselves. We should also do this together with other members of our church whom we trust. Have you been inviting brothers and sisters to speak into your life?

But Wait—One Last Thing!

There is one last thing we need to get squared away before we move on to the topic at hand. As we examine ourselves to see whether we are true Christians, it is absolutely essential that we keep our causes and effects straight. Otherwise, everything will get tangled.

Remember that God is the cause of our salvation. There is no doubt about that. You cannot save yourself by good works or hard effort. Remember, our natural state is spiritual death. We cannot do anything to bring ourselves to life.

Look carefully at what the apostle Paul says about our salvation in Ephesians 2:4–10:

> But God, being rich in mercy, because of the great love with which he loved us, even when we were dead in our trespasses, made us alive together with Christ—by grace you have been saved—and raised us up with him and seated us with him in the heavenly places in Christ Jesus, so that in the coming ages

he might show the immeasurable riches of his grace in kindness toward us in Christ Jesus. For by grace you have been saved through faith. And this is not your own doing; it is the gift of God, not a result of works, so that no one may boast. For we are his workmanship, created in Christ Jesus for good works, which God prepared beforehand, that we should walk in them.

Did you catch that? While we were dead in our sins, God made us alive. It was all his grace—a gift of God. In fact, God intentionally saves us in this way so that we will not boast or think that we have somehow saved ourselves (see Rom. 3:27)! God brings about our salvation. This means that the good works that we hope (and expect) to see in our lives can never be the cause of our salvation.

Instead, God's regenerating love and mercy is the cause. The fruit—growth in peace and love and faith and hatred for sin—are the results of what God does. They are the good works that he prepared for us, so that we can work out the implications of our salvation in the world.

Our goal in this book, in other words, is not to ask whether we have done enough to earn God's love and favor. Instead, our goal is to begin learning how to look for the evidence that God has done his mighty work in our lives. So let's get to work.

How to Respond

Reflect:

Before you read this chapter, how would you have defined a "Christian"? Has your definition changed at all?

What does the fact that we must be born again say about us?

What do you think might be the dangers in confusing the cause of our regeneration with the effects of our regeneration?

Repent:

Confess to God the truth that you are a sinner, completely deserving his just wrath.

If you have not already been "born again," ask God to give you that new life now.

Remember:

Think about Matthew 11:28–30: "Come to me, all who labor and are heavy laden, and I will give you rest. Take my yoke upon you, and learn from me, for I am gentle and lowly in heart, and you will find rest for your souls. For my yoke is easy, and my burden is light."

Each of us carries a heavy burden of sin, guilt, and shame. But Jesus invites each of us to come, no matter what we have done. And he promises rest and comfort to everyone who will come by faith.

Report:

Talk to a leader or friend in your church and ask for help in identifying any evidences that you have been born again.

3

You Are Not a Christian
Just Because You Like Jesus

IN 1966, JOHN LENNON created a stir by boasting—tongue in cheek—that the Beatles were "more popular than Jesus." Many were scandalized by Lennon's arrogance, but could it be that, at that moment in history, they were? The Beatles were in the middle of a decade-long run of worldwide success the likes of which have rarely been seen.

From a broader perspective, of course, Lennon's ride on the top was short lived. Only fifty years later his life and career have largely been relegated to the dustbin of nostalgia and curiosity, reduced to little more than the soundtracks for Nike commercials.

Jesus, on the other hand, continues to grow in popularity with every passing year, to say nothing of the fact that people have been talking about him for two thousand years. Weekly news magazines know that trotting out a painting of Jesus on their covers at Christmastime and Easter will sell extra copies. Movie producers know that films about Jesus often do well at the box office. In fact, the ability of Jesus's name to deliver at the cash register has spawned entire industries. Some of my favorites include:

1. The "What Would Jesus Eat?" Diet—for only $14.99 you can find out the long-hidden secret diet of the Messiah. My guess

is that he ate the same things every other first-century Pal-
estinian peasant ate: olives, fish, figs, bread, and Twizzlers
red licorice.

2. Flip-flops with the words "Jesus Loves You!" on the soles
so that you can leave an inspirational message in the sand
behind you. After all, people are always looking for hidden
messages in footprints at the beach.

3. A line of Jesus-themed pet clothing, including a dog shirt
that says "Jesus Ruffs Me" and another one that proclaims
"Jesus Fills My Dog Bowl." I'm not going to lie to you, I have
no idea what either of those means.

Jesus is even popular with people who aren't Christians. He
garners a lot of respect from the great men and women of other
faiths. The fourteenth Dalai Lama, one of the primary leaders
of Tibetan Buddhism, called Jesus "an enlightened person"
and heralded him as a master teacher.[1] Hindu leader Mahatma
Gandhi wrote warmly about Jesus, "The gentle figure of Christ,
so patient, so kind, so loving, so full of forgiveness that he
taught his followers not to retaliate when abused or struck, but
to turn the other cheek, I thought it was a beautiful example of
the perfect man."[2] The renowned scientist Albert Einstein once
told *The Saturday Evening Post*, "I am a Jew, but I am enthralled
by the luminous figure of the Nazarene [Jesus]. . . . No one can
read the Gospels without feeling the actual presence of Jesus.
His personality pulsates in every word. No myth is filled with
such life."[3] Even the Qur'an refers to Jesus as a prophet and
messenger of God.

What should we make of Jesus's popularity? It's not difficult
to understand that being a Christian means *liking* Jesus, and that
someone who *does not like* Jesus is probably not a Christian. But
can we say that liking him is enough to make you a Christian?
If Buddhists, Hindus, Muslims, and even atheists can think that
Jesus was a great guy, then certainly we cannot say that.

In the Gospel accounts of Jesus's life, time and again he encounters people who like him, respect him, and approve of what they perceive to be his message. But then he turns around and tells them that they are not his disciples, that they are missing something (e.g. John 3; Luke 9:57–62; Luke 18:18–22).

You Gotta Believe

You are not a Christian just because you like Jesus. Instead, being a Christian means that you believe in him. That is to say, you must have faith in him.

It's important for you to see this, so I don't want you to take my word for it. Consider what the Bible says. Here are just four of the many passages where the necessity of faith and belief are taught.

> For God so loved the world, that he gave his only Son, that who-ever *believes* in him should not perish but have eternal life. For God did not send his Son into the world to condemn the world, but in order that the world might be saved through him. Who-ever *believes* in him is not condemned, but whoever *does not believe* is condemned already, because he has not believed in the name of the only Son of God. . . . Whoever *believes* in the Son has eternal life. (John 3:16–18, 36)
>
> Then they said to him, "What must we do, to be doing the works of God?" Jesus answered them, "This is the work of God, *that you believe* in him whom he has sent." (John 6:28–29)
>
> But now the righteousness of God has been manifested apart from the law, although the Law and the Prophets bear witness to it—the righteousness of God through faith in Jesus Christ for all who believe. For there is no distinction: for all have sinned and fall short of the glory of God, and are justified by his grace as a gift, through the redemption that is in Christ Jesus, whom God put forward as a propitiation by his blood, *to be received by faith*." (Rom. 3:21–25)

> Without faith it is impossible to please him, for whoever would draw near to God *must believe* that he exists and that he rewards those who seek him. (Heb. 11:6)

It's pretty clear in passages like these that faith is essential to being a genuine Christian. Jesus says that eternal life comes through belief. Paul says the benefits of Christ's sacrificial death come by faith. And the author of Hebrews says that we are pleasing to God by faith.

Faith separates the true children of God from those who merely respect Jesus. You're not a Christian if you don't have faith in the Son of God. If you do have that faith, you are a Christian. Statements like these require greater clarification and qualification, of course, but they give you the broad outlines of what the Bible teaches.

What does the Bible mean by the word *faith*? We use the word faith to describe all kinds of things. We use it to describe religious systems, so that Muslims and Christians and Baha'is are all described as "people of faith." Or we talk of having faith that a certain stock will perform well in the coming year. A baseball team might be said to have faith in their closer when they turn the ball over to him in the ninth inning.

Sometimes people talk about faith as if it is the polar opposite of clear thinking or rational thought—faith as a state of certainty in the face of contradictory evidence. As a fan of the Philadelphia Eagles, I exercise this faith every season as I pick them to win the Super Bowl, even though they never, ever (ever!) do.

But that's not what Christian faith is like. The faith of a Christian, the faith that Jesus says marks the difference between eternal life and eternal condemnation, bears two essential elements: objective content and heartfelt trust.

Objective Content

In order to have faith, we must know certain facts about ourselves and about Jesus, who he is what he has done for us. Thus the apostle Paul asks rhetorically, "How are they to believe in him of whom they have never heard?" (Rom. 10:14). You cannot believe in something that you don't know about. Saving faith must have an object. You don't just believe; you believe *something*. And throughout Scripture we find essential truths that must be believed. Paul writes that we are saved through "belief in the truth" (2 Thess. 2:13). There are certain doctrines that people must hear, understand, and affirm if they want to become true Christians.

1) You Are a Sinner

The first truth you must believe, the first piece of content, is that you are a sinner. Jesus only accepts people who know they are sinners. To see that, consider how Jesus responds to people when they approach him. He usually responds in one of two ways. Some he receives with a warm and tender welcome. Others he sends away, sometimes with sharp words. What accounts for the difference?

Think about the story in Luke 5 in which Jesus calls a tax collector named Levi to be one of his disciples. Levi was so excited that he threw a huge party at his house so that Jesus could meet all of his tax collector friends. That might not seem like a big deal to you and me, but in those days, these people were scandalized. Tax collectors were the worst kind of sinners. They helped the occupying Roman government raise money, so they were traitors to their own people. They lined their pockets by collecting more taxes than necessary, so they were thieves and crooks. They made themselves rich at the expense of their neighbors and their nation. A tax collector was about as popular as a child molester would be nowadays.

In response to this scandalous calling of Levi, the Pharisees and the scribes said to Jesus's disciples, "Why do you eat and drink with tax collectors and sinners?" (Luke 5:30). It was a natural question. The Pharisees were the religious establishment. They were the good guys, the keepers of the rules. They were understandably dismayed by Jesus's decision to attend a dinner party with notorious sinners. But Jesus explained his actions to them, "Those who are well have no need of a physician, but those who are sick. I have not come to call the righteous but sinners to repentance" (Luke 5:31–32).

That's an extraordinary statement, isn't it? In another place, Jesus says that he came to seek and save the lost (Luke 19:10). Also extraordinary. We naturally expect that God will be nice to the good people and angry at the bad people. But here Jesus says that he has only come for those people who realize that they are sinners, that they are sick and need a physician.

In order to be a Christian, you must come to grips with your sinfulness and need for forgiveness. We must be poor in spirit (Matt. 5:3) and heed Jesus's call to repent. Every man, woman, and child on earth should cry out with the tax collector, "God, be merciful to me, a sinner!" (Luke 18:13).

Jesus's words about coming for the sick and sinful are both a comfort and a warning. On the one hand, Jesus promises to accept and heal anyone who comes to him in heartfelt repentance. That's good news for sinners like you and me. On the other hand, Jesus promises to reject anyone who tries to come to him without a sense of their own deep sinfulness. People who think they are already spiritually healthy will receive no healing from the Great Physician.

2) Jesus Is Fully God and Fully Man

In addition to believing something about yourself—that you are a sinner in need of forgiveness—being a Christian means that you must believe a few basic facts about who Jesus is. To begin with, you must believe that he is fully God and fully man.

Let's start with the idea that Jesus is fully God. In Romans 10 the apostle Paul tells us, "If you confess with your mouth that Jesus is Lord and believe in your heart that God raised him from the dead, you will be saved. For with the heart one believes and is justified, and with the mouth one confesses and is saved" (Rom. 10:9–10). In order to be saved you must confess with your mouth that Jesus is Lord. Here Paul's emphasis is not so much on the mode of confession (with your mouth) but on the content of our confession (Jesus is Lord). We must acknowledge, believe, confess, and proclaim that Jesus is Lord.

Now, I will say a few more things about the lordship of Jesus in a moment. But here I want to observe that the confession "Jesus is Lord" is, among other things, a confession of Jesus's divinity—his divine nature. Think of Doubting Thomas bowing before the resurrected Jesus and saying, "My Lord and my God" (John 20:28). Once the apostles realized that Jesus was God, the term *Lord* became imbued with Christ's divinity. Paul also refers to Jesus as Lord in such a way as to clarify that he considers Jesus to be God himself. New Testament scholar Larry Hurtado suggests that to "'call upon the name of the Lord' is a frequent biblical expression for the worship of *Yahweh*."[4] So the Apostle often quotes Old Testament passages that are speaking about God and applies them directly to the Lord Jesus.[5] The divinity of Jesus is an essential Christian doctrine because only an infinite and sinless person could take the infinite punishment that our sins deserve. If Jesus is not God, he cannot save us.

Yet we must also believe that Jesus is fully man. Some people in the early Christian church struggled less with the idea of Jesus's divinity and more with the idea of his humanity. They believed that God had come to them in the person of Jesus Christ. However, they could not imagine that God could fully take on human flesh, live as a human being, and suffer and die as a man. It just seemed like too much. How could God possibly stoop that low?

To address that confusion, the apostle John wrote a clarifying statement for the church: "By this you know the Spirit of God: every spirit that confesses that Jesus Christ has come in the flesh is from God, and every spirit that does not confess Jesus is not from God. This is the spirit of the antichrist, which you heard was coming and now is in the world already" (1 John 4:2–3). Just as Jesus can only save us if he is fully divine, so he can only save us if he is fully human. Only a human can stand in the place of another human, taking the punishment we deserve. Only a member of the human race could undo the curse that Adam had brought on us (Rom. 5:12–21). Only one who knew the frailty and weakness of being a man could be a sympathetic and merciful priest for us (Heb. 4:14–16).

So a Christian is someone who confesses both Jesus's divinity and humanity. The New Testament authors are unable to imagine any formulation of Christianity that rejects those beliefs.

3) Jesus the God-Man Saves through His Death

To be a Christian means believing something about who Jesus is, but it also means believing something about what he came to do. You must believe Jesus is the God-man, and you must believe that he is the God-man who came to seek and save the lost by dying on the cross and rising again. This brings us to the very heart of Christianity. Let's start by considering the cross.

On the cross, Jesus bore the curse of death that our sins deserve (Gal. 3:13). On the cross he took the wrath of God that our sins deserve (Rom. 3:24–25). On the cross Jesus took the blame and guilt that our sins deserve so that now there is no condemnation left for us (2 Cor. 5:21; Rom. 8:1).

When we look at the apostolic preaching in the book of Acts, we see that they proclaimed the crucifixion of Christ as an essential part of the Christian message (e.g., Acts 2:23; 3:15; 4:10; 26:22–23). The death of Christ is so central to Christianity that Paul can even refer to the entire Christian proclamation as the "word of the cross" (1 Cor. 1:18). Because this is true, genuine followers of Christ must believe that Jesus's death is sufficient to save them from their sins. We must be able to say along with the apostle Paul, "The life I now live in the flesh I live by faith in the Son of God, *who loved me and gave himself for me*" (Gal. 2:20).

The late Leon Morris wrote, "To put it bluntly and plainly, if Christ is not my Substitute, I still occupy the place of a condemned sinner. If my sins and my guilt are not transferred to Him, if He did not take them upon Himself, then surely they remain with me. If He did not deal with my sins, I must face their consequences. If my penalty was not borne by Him, it still hangs over me."[6] Every believer in Christ must affirm the truth that Christ died a sacrificial death in the place of sinners.

4) Jesus Was Raised Bodily from the Dead

The resurrection of Christ doesn't get all of the attention that the crucifixion gets. Christians are sometimes guilty of treating it as some sort of cosmic happy ending to the passion narrative. But there's no doubt that believing in the resurrection is also at the center of what you must do to be a Christian. Remember Paul's words: "If you confess with your mouth that Jesus is Lord and believe in your heart that God raised him from the dead, you will be saved" (Rom. 10:9). Christ's resurrection was essential to our salvation. Paul wrote elsewhere, "If Christ has not been raised, then our preaching is in vain and your faith is in vain" (1 Cor. 15:14).

Why was it essential? My friend Sam Allberry describes the resurrection as God's signature on Christ's work and our salvation.[7] You might think of the way the FedEx delivery man comes to your door and asks you to sign for a package. Your signature shows that you accept the parcel and that the transaction has been completed to your satisfaction. In the same way, God shows his satisfaction with Christ's suffering and death by raising him from the dead (see Peter's argument in Acts 2:22–36). The resurrection of Christ shows that Jesus is who he said he is and that he accomplishes the salvation he came to secure. If there were no resurrection, then Jesus would still be in the tomb, unable to help, save, and mediate for us.

The resurrection of Christ is of first importance. It's at the very heart of the salvation Christ offers to his people. As Paul tells us, "For I delivered to you as of first importance what I also received: that Christ died for our sins in accordance with the Scriptures, that he was buried, that he was raised on the third day in accordance with the Scriptures" (1 Cor. 15:3–4). If you believe in your heart that God raised Jesus from the dead, you will be saved.

5) Jesus Is Lord

There's one more piece of content that you must believe to be a Christian. You must believe that he is the only right Lord. You must believe he is Lord because he is God and he created the world, yes, but you must also believe that he is your Lord—or supreme authority—because he has redeemed you for himself as one of his people.

After his crucifixion and resurrection, Jesus declares that "All authority in heaven and on earth has been given to me" (Matt. 28:18). The divine Son submitted to the divine Father to the utmost, and so the Father "put all things in subjection under his feet" (1 Cor. 15:27). The Father exalted the Son (see Heb. 1:8–9). The crucified one, says Peter, is the Lord and Christ (Acts 2:36).

The apostle Paul puts the divinity, humanity, suffering, resurrection, and authority of Jesus together in one glorious statement:

> And being found in human form, he humbled himself by becoming obedient to the point of death, even death on a cross. Therefore God has highly exalted him and bestowed on him the name that is above every name, so that at the name of Jesus every knee should bow, in heaven and on earth and under the earth, and every tongue confess that Jesus Christ is Lord, to the glory of God the Father." (Phil. 2:8–11)

To call Jesus your Lord is to say that he has authority over your life and is worthy of your obedience. If we call him "Lord, Lord," we must be willing to do what he says (Luke 6:46). He is the head of his church (Eph. 5:22–24) and will one day return to have his lordship acknowledged by all people.

The question for you is whether you agree that all five of these statements above are true. If not, the Bible is clear that you are not a genuine Christian. As one author states it, "Those who reject these foundational doctrines of the Christian faith cannot be saved, no matter how swell they are and how well they behave. Being good is not enough. We must know and believe something—the basic facts about salvation—to be saved."[8]

But What about Doubt?

Does this mean that a true Christian's faith never wavers? No, it doesn't mean that. Should you conclude that you are not a Christian if you sometimes have periods when you struggle to believe? Again, no. Can a genuine believer sometimes struggle with doubt? Yes, many have and many do.

- Abraham believed the Lord's promise of a child in his old age (Gen. 15:6), but later on he doubted (Gen. 17:17).
- Gideon is heralded as a champion of faith (Heb. 11:32), but when the Lord promised to deliver Israel through him he required not one but two miraculous confirmations before he would believe.
- John the Baptist knew that Jesus was God's Messiah (John 1:29), but he began to wonder if he had been wrong when he was sitting in prison and Jesus didn't seem to be doing much to overthrow evildoers (Luke 7:19–20).
- Peter walked on water until the wind grew stronger. His doubts began to crowd out his faith in Jesus's power to keep him dry (Matt. 14:28–31).

Even outside the pages of Scripture, Augustine, Martin Luther, William Cowper, and millions of other Christians have struggled at different times and in different degrees with fear and doubt. If we are honest, there are times when all of the facts seem to contradict the Word of God, and our nerve fails.

It's at those moments that we need to be in close connection with other brothers and sisters in a local congregation. When our sight is momentarily dim, we need others who can see more clearly to help us fight through doubt. When faced with these kinds of struggles, Christians do not merely jettison doctrines of the faith. We instead encourage each other to trust the Word and wisdom of God and cry out like the man who cried out to Jesus, "I believe; help my unbelief!" (Mark 9:24).

Doubt is a common experience for true believers. Still, if we want to be faithful to the Bible's teaching, we must insist that there is a body of objective doctrine that must be believed by anyone who is a genuine Christian. This is where we part company with our friends from other faiths, self-made faiths, or no faith at all, even if they respect Jesus as a prophet or a great teacher. Many people enjoy Christ's teaching in the Beatitudes. But the more telling matter is whether they believe that the man teaching those principles was actually God in flesh who would later die for the sins of his people and rise from the dead and become their Lord.

Heartfelt Trust

I've spent the bulk of this chapter arguing that a true Christian must believe in the factual truth of certain propositions. But I must also be clear that biblical belief or faith is more than intellectual assent to a set of truth propositions. Biblical belief or faith is a personal, heartfelt trust in a person.

The difference between these two kinds of belief isn't too hard to see. Intellectual assent is like a sideways nod of the head to someone passing by while you continue on your merry way. A personal, heartfelt trust, however, means changing the direction in which you're walking. Someone you love and trust has asked you to follow, and so you do. Heartfelt trust yields a happy obedience.

The book of James makes this distinction super clear. James writes, "You believe that God is one; you do well. Even the demons believe—and shudder!" (James 2:19). Even demons have what theologians call a "historical faith." They know that Jesus is the Son of God (and came to destroy them; see Mark 1:24 and Luke 4:41). But they hate those facts. They oppose them and do everything they can to undermine these realities. A person with truth faith, on the other hand, shows his faith by his works (James 2:22–23).

It's not only demons, of course, who have this kind of deficient faith. It's people, too. In John's Gospel, John tells of the crowds who saw Jesus's miracles and believed in his name. But then he tells us that "Jesus on his part did not entrust himself to them, because he knew all people and needed no one to bear witness about man, for he himself knew what was in man" (John 2:24–25). The crowds had seen enough of Jesus's power to know that he was sent from God (cf. Nicodemus's statement a few verses later in John 3:2). But they lacked a deeper commitment and trust in Jesus. Jesus, knowing the true state of their hearts, did not trust them.

You are not a Christian just because you like Jesus. You must believe *in* Jesus, as John 3:16 put it. It's not enough to simply believe things *about* Jesus. You must believe that you need a Savior, and that he is that Savior. You must believe that you need a Lord, and that he is that Lord.

Our confidence must not merely be in things that once happened, but in the person who accomplished them. When we come to Jesus in trust for the forgiveness and healing that we so desperately need, we find that he is willing and able to help us.

How to Respond

Reflect:

> How would you respond to someone who argues that true Christianity is not a set of religious dogmas that we must affirm, but instead is a call to be gentle and loving and generous as Jesus was?

> Do you affirm the historical truth of each one of the five points of doctrine discussed in this chapter? If not, what do you think that says about whether you are truly a Christian?

> Do you find it difficult to trust Jesus for the salvation and forgiveness that he has promised? What false "gods" have you trusted?

> In John 6:40 Jesus says, "For this is the will of my Father, that everyone who looks on the Son and believes in him should

have eternal life, and I will raise him up on the last day." What do you think it means to "look on the Son and believe in him"?

Repent:

Ask God to forgive you for your unbelief and your trust in other "gods."

Think of a concrete step you could take toward strengthening your faith and trust in Jesus alone.

Remember:

Think about 1 John 1:9: "If we confess our sins, he is faithful and just to forgive us our sins and to cleanse us from all unrighteousness."

No matter how hard you try, you cannot do enough to earn God's favor. But the good news is that Jesus has done everything on our behalf. Thank God that he is faithful to forgive all who come to him through faith in Christ, no matter what they have done.

Report:

Talk to a leader or friend in your church and ask for help in growing in your understanding of and trust in Jesus.

4

You Are Not a Christian
If You Enjoy Sin

REGGIE WHITE played college football at the University of Tennessee. While he was there, he set school records for most sacks in a career, most sacks in a season, and most sacks in a game. Almost thirty years later, those records still stand. He spent two seasons in the now-defunct USFL, and then joined my team, the Philadelphia Eagles, in 1985. Over the next eight years White recorded 124 sacks, more than one sack per game, while establishing all sorts of franchise records. He was the greatest player in Eagles history and my favorite player ever.

He also betrayed me.

Well, that's not entirely fair. White was granted free agency in 1993 by the National Football League, making him able to sign with any team he liked. Over two thousand Eagles fans rallied to JFK Plaza in downtown Philadelphia and tried to pressure Eagles' ownership into re-signing the star lineman. But White would eventually sign for a massive amount of money with the Green Bay Packers without ever receiving a contract offer from the Eagles.

An objective observer (which I am not) would say that he made the right decision. He received a lot of money and would eventually win a Super Bowl in Green Bay, two things that would never have happened under any circumstances had he remained in Philadelphia.

Still, it killed me to watch on television as White lined up as a Packer for the first time. He was supposed to be an Eagle. He had worn the kelly green and silver through so many battles. Eagles fans had pinned their hope on him for so many Sundays. But now he was wearing garish yellow pants while a bunch of cheese-eating Packer fans cheered as if he was one of *theirs*. It was the visual equivalent of fingernails on a chalkboard; I turned the TV off in disgust.

Almost twenty years later, the pain is finally fading. In fact, as I sit here writing at my desk, I am wearing a throwback Eagles number 92 T-shirt with "WHITE" emblazoned across the back. Time heals all wounds, I suppose.

What does any of this have to do with whether you are really a Christian? Well, I think the question of what jersey you're wearing helps us think about sin in the life of a professing Christian. To call yourself a Christian is to say you've changed teams. It's to put on a new jersey that says to everyone that you have new allegiances. But what would you think of someone who put on a new jersey but kept playing for the old team? That's what we're doing as Christians whenever we sin. We're playing for the old team even though we're wearing the new jersey. Sin for someone who claims to be a Christian is a strange kind of treason. It is taking Satan's side in rebellion against God even though you're saying you're on God's side.

Don't misunderstand. All Christians continue to struggle with sin. But the Bible also suggests that if your life continues to be characterized by a casual and comfortable attitude toward sin, you should stop and think about what you really are. Never mind what jersey you think you're wearing. Who are you really playing for? If it's mostly for the other team, maybe you really belong to their roster, after all. Here's another way to put it: you are not a Christian if you love sin. That's what we're going to think about in this chapter.

Sons of Satan and Sons of Salvation

Nowhere is this reality clearer than in 1 John 3. The apostle doesn't use the image of a team but instead the image of a family. Some people are God's children, he says. God is their Father and they are part of his family. Other people are children of the Devil. They belong to Satan and are part of his people. One way we can determine which family we belong to is by taking stock of the sin in our life. Take a minute to read this passage slowly:

> See what kind of love the Father has given to us, that we should be called *children of God*; and so we are. The reason why the world does not know us is that it did not know him. Beloved, *we are God's children now*, and what we will be has not yet appeared; but we know that when he appears we shall be like him, because we shall see him as he is. And everyone who thus hopes in him purifies himself as he is pure.
>
> Everyone who makes a practice of sinning also practices lawlessness; sin is lawlessness. You know that he appeared to take away sins, and in him there is no sin. No one who abides in him keeps on sinning; no one who keeps on sinning has either seen him or known him. Little children, let no one deceive you. Whoever practices righteousness is righteous, as he is righteous. Whoever makes a practice of sinning is of the devil, for the devil has been sinning from the beginning. The reason the Son of God appeared was to destroy the works of the devil. No one *born of God* makes a practice of sinning, for God's seed abides in him, and he cannot keep on sinning because he has been *born of God*. By this it is evident who are *the children of God*, and who are *the children of the devil*: whoever does not practice righteousness is not of God. (1 John 3:1–10a)

Sin is the Devil's specialty. He is God's enemy, and he's been "sinning from the beginning," says John. Since the garden of Eden, Satan has been busy spreading sin throughout the world God created. He lied and tempted Adam and Eve to rebel against God's authority. This sin spread to the next generation, and Cain murdered Abel. By the time we get to Genesis 6, we learn that, "The LORD saw that the wickedness of man was great in the earth, and that every intention of the thoughts of his heart was only evil continually" (v. 5). Within a few short chapters of Genesis, we have taken a roller-coaster ride from a creation that pleases God to a creation that God wants to destroy (Gen. 1:31; 6:7). That is the fruit of Satan's labor. He has been sinning from the beginning; he is still sinning today.

The arrival of Jesus was God's great blow to his adversary. "The reason the Son of God appeared," we just read, "was to destroy the works of the devil" (1 John 3:8). Another way to say this is to say, "He appeared to take away sins" (1 John 3:5). And the Bible tells us that he was successful in doing just that. By his atoning death Jesus dealt with the problem of sin. He had no sin of his own to pay for (v. 5), which allowed him to take the sins of his people on himself and pay for them completely. There is now no condemnation for those who are in Christ Jesus because Jesus was fully condemned in our place (Rom. 8:1). Satan no longer has any basis on which to accuse us before God because our sins have been wiped away (1 John 1:7; Rev. 12:10).

Since our sins have been blotted out, we are no longer children of the Devil. We have been granted a new identity, a new family. So John instructs us to marvel at God's kindness: "See what kind of love the Father has given to us, that we should be called children of God; and so we are" (1 John 3:1). We are no longer Satan's. We belong to God. We are no longer trapped in the domain of darkness but have been called into his marvelous light (1 Pet. 2:9, Col. 1:13–14). We are no longer under the power of Satan but are under the power of God (Acts 26:17–18). We were once children of wrath but now are children of God (Eph. 2:3). Being a Christian involves a radical change of identity.

You Do What You Are

Okay, admit it. You didn't read that last part very closely. You skimmed it, didn't you? It's okay, you can tell the truth; it's just you and me here (and I'm not even really here, am I?). All right, I like the cut of your jib, so I'm going to cut you a break. Let me summarize for you what you need to know. The Bible says that there are two kinds of people: servants of Satan and servants of God. It's one jersey or the other. And the way you can tell which jersey you're wearing is by the role that sin plays in your life.

Sin Characterizes Satan's Children

"Whoever makes a practice of sinning is of the devil," we heard John say (1 John 3:8). Sin is the distinguishing mark of the Devil's child. Like a brand on a cow, it's a mark of ownership. John even makes the point a second time with slightly different words: "By this it is evident who are the children of God, and who are the children of the devil: whoever does not practice righteousness is not of God" (1 John 3:10). The children of the Devil make a practice of sinning because that's what their father the Devil does. There's no way around it: it's a family resemblance. Before we become followers of Christ, we are all slaves to sin. We cannot do otherwise because sin is part of who we are.[1]

In his Gospel, John recounts an episode with Jesus that teaches the same thing. Jesus explains to a crowd of people, "You are of your father the devil, and your will is to do your father's desires. He was a murderer from the beginning, and has nothing to do with the truth, because there is no truth in him. When he lies, he speaks out of his own character, for he is a liar and the father of lies" (John 8:44). The crowds were sinning because they wanted to do their father's desires.

Sin's Power over God's Children Is Broken

Just the opposite is true of a Christian. When we are transferred from Satan's family and adopted into God's family, our relationship to sin changes. Before, we were motivated and controlled by the desire for sin. Now, we live by God's Spirit. Sin does not have the same power to energize or move us. Its power is broken.

In his letter to the church at Rome, Paul explains that sin's power is broken because of Christ's death. He writes, "We know that our old self was crucified with him in order that the body of sin might be brought to nothing, so that we would no longer be enslaved to sin" (Rom. 6:6). The old person has been crucified with Christ. The old slave of sin is dead.

In its place is a new man, a man that is dead with respect to sin but alive with respect to God. Paul continues,

> Consider yourselves dead to sin and alive to God in Christ Jesus.
>
> Let not sin therefore reign in your mortal body, to make you obey its passions. Do not present your members to sin as instruments for unrighteousness, but present yourselves to God as those who have been brought from death to life, and your members to God as instruments for righteousness. For sin will have no dominion over you, since you are not under law but under grace. (Rom. 6:11–14)

Sin is inconsistent with the reality of the Christian's identity. A Christian, remember, is someone who has switched teams. So when Paul tells Christians not to sin, he is not saying, "Pretend to be something you're not." Just the opposite—he is saying, "Play for the team that has actually placed you on its roster!" Paul wants Christians to *do* in daily life what they already *are* in Jesus. So the Apostle asks rhetorically, "How can we who died to sin still live in it?" (Rom. 6:2).

A New Obedience

The Christian has a new controlling principle. The controlling principle is no longer sin. It's what Thomas Schreiner calls "a new obedience."[2] Christians are not saved or justified by this new obedience, but their salvation will manifest itself in concrete ways—in this new obedience.

What does this new obedience look like? Positively, it looks like new fruit which begins to appear. Negatively, it looks like forsaking old sins. Here's Paul describing both sides: "But the fruit of the Spirit is love, joy, peace, patience, kindness, goodness, faithfulness, gentleness, self-control; against such things there is no law. And those who belong to Christ Jesus have crucified the flesh with its passions and desires" (Gal. 5:22–24). Notice how straightforward these final words are. Those who belong to Christ *have crucified the flesh*. They have done it. Or at least we can say they are doing it. On the flip side, the Spirit is giving new fruit: love, peace, patience, and so on.

True Christianity *changes* people. You must understand this. Christ appeared to take away sins, and he came to destroy the works of the Evil One. That means there is no way to be a Christian and to continue loving the things that Christ hates and came to destroy. There is no way to be a child of God and to continue embracing the sin which pleases the Devil.

This is why Scripture regularly warns those who continue to sin happily and complacently. Listen to these warnings:

Or do you not know that the unrighteous will not inherit the kingdom of God? *Do not be deceived*: neither the sexually immoral, nor idolaters, nor adulterers, nor men who practice homosexuality, nor thieves, nor the greedy, nor drunkards, nor revilers, nor swindlers will inherit the kingdom of God. (1 Cor. 6:9–10)

Now the works of the flesh are evident: sexual immorality, impurity, sensuality, idolatry, sorcery, enmity, strife, jealousy, fits of anger, rivalries, dissensions, divisions, envy, drunkenness, orgies, and things like these. *I warn you, as I warned you before*, that those who do such things will not inherit the kingdom of God. (Gal. 5:19–21)

For you may be sure of this, that everyone who is sexually immoral or impure, or who is covetous (that is, an idolater), has no inheritance in the kingdom of Christ and God. *Let no one deceive you with empty words*, for because of these things the wrath of God comes upon the sons of disobedience. (Eph. 5:5–6)

Did you notice that each one of those passages specifically advises you and me to not ignore its warning? Paul knows us pretty well. He's concerned that we will be deceived, or will let someone else convince us otherwise, or will forget his admonishment. Our hearts oftentimes want to make excuses and pretend that none of this is true. So these passages are meant to be flashing red lights: "Don't go this way!" Sin is incompatible with the Christian's new identity. Sinners will not inherit God's kingdom.

John sums all this up by handing out a new obedience test. Take this test by yourself or with a friend. Take it at church or at home. Either way, here's John's test:

Whoever says "I know him" but does not keep his commandments is a liar, and the truth is not in him, but whoever keeps his word, in him truly the love of God is perfected. By this we may know that we are in him: whoever says he abides in him ought to walk in the same way in which he walked." (1 John 2:4–6)

The test is for anyone who says, "I know him." Is that you? And the test is pretty straightforward. It just has one question: Do you keep Christ's Word and walk in the same way he walked? If not, then you need to go back and look at Paul's warnings which are listed above. They are especially relevant for you.

Ummm . . . But Doesn't Everyone Sin?

If Christ calls his people to a new obedience, one obvious question follows: Who can possibly be a Christian since everyone sins? Anyone with even the slightest shred of self-awareness knows that he or she sins all the time. Christians struggle with every kind of sin imaginable. Off the top of my head I can think of specific moments in which I have been irritable, selfish, lazy, proud, and greedy. And that's just in the last four hours.[3]

Well, nowhere does the Bible suggest that a believer will live life free from sin. In fact John tells us explicitly, "If we say we have no sin, we deceive ourselves, and the truth is not in us. . . . If we say we have not sinned, we make him a liar, and his word is not in us" (1 John 1:8–10). Apparently, there were false teachers in the early church who claimed that they had not sinned since becoming followers of Christ.[4] These teachers were self-deceived and, what's more, were implicitly claiming that God himself was a liar since God says that everyone sins.

So how do we put these pieces together? On one hand, the Bible says that Christians are dead to sin and free from its power. It says they are alive to Christ and empowered by his Spirit to bear the good fruit of obedience. It says that sin is incompatible with our new identity as sons and daughters of God. On the other hand, Scripture says that anyone who claims that he or she does not sin is a liar. So is the Bible contradicting itself? What gives?

Let's look more closely at what 1 John 3 actually says. Remember, we read there that:

- no one who abides in him keeps on sinning (verse 6);
- no one who keeps on sinning has either seen him or known him (verse 6);
- whoever makes a practice of sinning is of the Devil (verse 8);
- no one born of God makes a practice of sinning (verse 9);
- he cannot keep on sinning because he has been born of God (verse 9);
- whoever does not practice righteousness is not of God (verse 10).

Now, I don't normally find myself terribly excited about ancient Greek verb tenses, but we're talking about the difference between heaven and hell, so I'll make an exception. The verbs in each of these examples are in the present tense: "abides," "keeps on," "makes a practice," and so forth. All these verbs point to *ongoing and continuous action*. John is not saying anything about the Christian who falls into sin. Rather, he's talking about the person whose life trajectory is characterized by it. He's talking about the person who, you might say, consciously *abides* in it, deliberately *keeps* in it, and happily *makes it a practice.*

The pattern and direction of a Christian's day-in, day-out conduct will reflect a desire to love and obey Jesus, not Satan. A Christian cannot be characterized by a lifestyle of sin.

How Can You Tell?

Both Christians and non-Christians sin every day. Both struggle to break bad habits and overcome patterns of weakness and failure. And I cannot say that Christians are the best people on earth in terms of aggregate sins. You could look at a given day in the life of a non-Christian, and you might see less selfishness, less anger, less pettiness, and less pride than you would see in that same day in the life of a Christian. So how can we tell the difference between a real Christian and someone who claims to be a Christian but is deceived?

To answer that, let's look to one of Jesus's parables:

There was a man who had two sons. And the younger of them said to his father, "Father, give me the share of property that is coming to me." And he divided his property between them. Not many days later, the younger son gathered all he had and took a journey into a far country, and there he squandered his property in reckless living. And when he had spent everything, a severe famine arose in that country, and he began to be in need. So he went and hired himself out to one of the citizens of that country, who sent him into his fields to feed pigs. And he was longing to be fed with the pods that the pigs ate, and no one gave him anything.

But when he came to himself, he said, "How many of my father's hired servants have more than enough bread, but I perish here with hunger! I will arise and go to my father, and I will say to him, 'Father, I have sinned against heaven and before you. I am no longer worthy to be called your son. Treat me as one of your hired servants.'" And he arose and came to his father. But while he was still a long way off, his father saw him and felt compassion, and ran and embraced him and kissed him. And the son said to him, "Father, I have sinned against heaven and before you. I am no longer worthy to be called your son." But the father said to his servants, "Bring quickly the best robe, and put it on him, and put a ring on his hand, and shoes on his feet. And bring the fattened calf and kill it, and let us eat and celebrate. For this my son was dead, and is alive again; he was lost, and is found." And they began to celebrate.[5] (Luke 15:11–24)

This parable is particularly helpful to us as we think about how a Christian responds to sin. This young man was a sinner.

He insulted his father, squandered his inheritance on riotous living, and found himself in the gutter. That is a situation in which too many Christians have found themselves. But three things characterize the Prodigal Son's response to his sin, and they must characterize the response of anyone who is a true believer.

Revulsion

The son's turnaround began when he saw the reality of his sin clearly. He realized what a fool he had been, how offensive his behavior and attitudes were, and how ratty the pleasures of sin were in comparison to the joys of his father's home. In Jesus's words, "he came to himself"—he came to his senses.

Since a Christian is dead to sin and alive to Christ, when he does sin, he finds that it doesn't suit him. He cannot be comfortable living in it. Although sin may provide him with a moment of pleasure and enjoyment, he is later plagued with feelings of regret, disappointment, and shame. If a true follower of Jesus is snared in sin, he will eventually have a moment like the Prodigal Son had in the pigsty where he comes to hate his sin. He does not grow in an ever-increasing love for sin, but as time goes by, he hates it.

Repentance

When the son came to his senses, he gave up his folly and returned home. What a wonderful picture of repentance! Genuine repentance is more than feeling badly or admitting we were wrong. It's even more than confessing our guilt. It involves turning away from sin and turning toward Jesus in faith with the resolution to obey him. Christians must renounce and condemn our sinful behaviors and commit ourselves to a wholehearted obedience to Jesus.

Reproof

No true Christian can ultimately prosper in sin. The heavenly Father, with great kindness, refuses to let one of his children become comfortable in rebellion. Just as the famine helped the Prodigal Son hit rock bottom and come to his senses, so the Lord will lovingly send circumstances, opportunities, difficulties, and correction to help his children repent and leave their sin.

The book of Hebrews tells us that this discipline is one of the ways we can know that we are God's children:

> It is for discipline that you have to endure. God is treating you as sons. For what son is there whom his father does not discipline? If you are left without discipline, in which all have participated, then you are illegitimate children and not sons. Besides this, we have had earthly fathers who disciplined us and we respected them. Shall we not much more be subject to the Father of spirits and live? For they disciplined us for a short time as it seemed best to them, but he disciplines us for our good, that we may share his holiness. For the moment all discipline seems painful rather than pleasant, but later it yields the peaceful fruit of righteousness to those who have been trained by it. (Heb. 12:7–11)

God disciplines his people because he loves them too much to leave them in their sin.

We are all sinners. Each of us has done more than enough to earn an eternity in hell. And none of us will achieve holiness on this side of eternity. But don't be deceived—a true Christian cannot continue in an unbroken trajectory of sin. There must be evidence of genuine revulsion, repentance, and reproof.

Not an Exact Science

So are you a Christian or a false professor? Admittedly, there is not an exact science for answering that question. It's not about determining how much sin you can commit and still be a Christian—ten sins a day puts you in the yellow zone, twenty sins, the red zone, etc. It's not about going through certain rituals after you sin in order to secure God's forgiveness—read Psalm 51, pray this prayer, and you're clean!

Instead, it involves things that are much more difficult to evaluate: the attitudes of the heart and the intentions and commitments of your soul. This is the reason why the Christian life should be lived out with other brothers and sisters in a faithful local church. We are not good judges of our own hearts. Some people are entirely too easy on themselves. They imagine that they give evidence of genuine regret and repentance for their sin when in reality there is none. Others with a tender conscience are far too hard on themselves. They take every weakness and failure as evidence that they are hypocrites and false Christians.

Being involved in a local church is immensely helpful for both kinds of people in at least three ways. First, sitting under the preaching of God's Word helps to align our values and measurements with God's. As we discover what *God means* by holiness, we become less enamored with our *own ideas* of righteousness and unrighteousness. Hearing from the Word teaches us what pleases God and what doesn't.

Second, watching the example of other believers makes obedience to God seem normal and possible in a world where sin is normally accepted and even celebrated. Third, letting other Christians know us (our attitudes, our conduct, our struggles) gives them the opportunity to speak into our lives. That way, they can warn us about worrisome patterns of sin or encourage us when we are feeling overwhelmed by our struggles. They help us to locate our blind spots.

A Great Savior

In this chapter, we walk a fine line. We must maintain the scriptural balance between the reality of God's great holiness and God's amazing mercy. So on the one hand, I fear for those who are not genuine Christians and are self-deceived, missing what their lifestyles of sin say about their professions of faith. If that is you, I hope this chapter has made you very uncomfortable.

On the other hand, I'm concerned for those who are genuine Christians struggling against sin, but who will be tempted to think of God as harsh and ready to spring on them every time they fail. If that is you, remember the kindness that Jesus shows to his people. His death is sufficient to wipe away all your guilt and make you new. When you fall into sin, run to Jesus. As we read in the book of Hebrews, "We do not have a high priest who is unable to sympathize with our weaknesses, but one who in every respect has been tempted as we are, yet without sin. Let us then with confidence draw near to the throne of grace, that we may receive mercy and find grace to help in time of need" (4:15–16).

But here's the bottom line: by calling yourself a Christian, you've put on the Christian jersey. Yet whose team are you really playing for—your own or Christ's? What would your closest family members, friends, and fellow church members say?

How to Respond

Reflect:

What is the connection between spiritual identity and attitude toward sin?

If God is merciful and quick to forgive, then why does it matter if we sin?

If someone claimed to be a Christian but did not have any interest in resisting sin and growing in holiness, what would the Bible say to that person?

When was the last time you did something or did not do something simply because you love God and desire to obey him?

Have you seen evidence of revulsion, repentance, and reproof in your life?

Repent:

Ask God to forgive you for your sins, especially sins that you have practiced over a long time. Think of a concrete step you could take toward changing your behavior.

Remember:

Read John 3:16: "For God so loved the world, that he gave his only Son, that whoever believes in him should not perish but have eternal life."

Praise God that he grants eternal life to everyone who believes in Jesus. You cannot earn salvation by living a holy life; you can only be saved by turning to Christ and trusting him for what he has done for you.

Report:

Talk to a leader or friend in your church and discuss your struggle with sin. Ask that person to help you grow and keep you accountable.

5

You Are Not a Christian
If You Do Not Endure to the End

MY LOVELY WIFE, KAREN, is the toughest person I have ever met. I can say with confidence that you have never met anyone with a higher pain tolerance than hers. How tough is she? Thanks for asking. She's so tough that she gave birth to our fourth child via C-section with no anesthesia—by request. Let that sink in for a second.

Karen also loves to run. Before we had children, she had a checklist of running-related goals to accomplish before taking on the responsibilities of motherhood. She spent one summer running trails in the Rocky Mountains and entering high-altitude half marathons. When she returned home to Philadelphia, she began training for the Philadelphia Marathon.

Being the amazing husband that I am, I wanted to encourage her by training with her. After all, it's easier to achieve a goal when someone is sharing the experience with you. There was only one problem: I hate running. Well, that's not entirely true. I hate running for more than a few minutes. I prefer the kind of running you do in baseball: run for five seconds, then stand still for five minutes. But running for the sake of running? Running for a really, really long time without stopping? And then, for all your effort, ending up at the same place?

Still, four times a week Karen and I and our dog would head

out on the trail that runs along the river from Valley Forge Park into the city. After twenty minutes, I began to actively dislike what I was doing. After thirty minutes, I hated it. After forty minutes, I wanted to curl up on the side of the road. By forty-five minutes, I was praying for sweet death. After an hour, I would head home to ice my quads.

About an hour and a half later, Karen would run by the house and drop off the dog, which looked like I felt. Another hour and a half later, Karen would come home, sweaty but unnervingly chipper for someone who just ran for four hours.

What was the difference between us? Endurance. She had it; I didn't. When things got tough on the trail, I quit. Karen kept running through the pain and difficulty.

Well, physical endurance is nice, if you have it. But the Bible talks about another kind of endurance that is far more important: spiritual endurance. A true Christian *must* and *will* remain in the faith until the end, whether the end is death or Christ's return. Here's how Jesus puts it: "But the one who endures to the end will be saved" (Matt. 10:22).

Now, the illustration about my wife's physical endurance only goes so far. Spiritual endurance involves our work of endurance, yes, but it also depends on God's enduring work. More on that in a moment. In the meantime, let's start with this one basic idea: if you do not endure until the end, you are not a Christian.

The Missing Millions

A quick search on the Internet will turn up dozens of websites run by "ex-Christians" who have seen the light and abandoned the faith, usually with some anger.[1] Most people who walk away from the faith, however, do so more quietly—and often unconsciously. Once upon a time, they prayed a prayer, signed a card, or walked an aisle. They were baptized, joined a church, and made a decent start of it. They cleaned up their act, tried to be good, and attended church on Sundays. But . . . then . . . they stopped. They turned their focus. Maybe it happened suddenly, or maybe slowly and imperceptibly. But it happened.

What caused the turning? It could have been any number of things. Maybe certain standards of behavior seemed unrealistic. Or certain doctrines seemed unlikely. Or the Christian road seemed unappealing. Or other things began looking more attractive. The point is that they stopped pursuing Christ. They quit running and went home. They didn't hold a press conference or announce it on Facebook. Some of them might even still call themselves Christians if you pressed them. But for one reason or another, they effectively stopped being Christians.

This silent exodus from the faith can be seen in the statistics gathered by the Southern Baptist Convention (SBC), the largest Baptist group in the United States. In 2004, there were over sixteen million members spread across over forty-three thousand churches. Sixteen million people were baptized after professing Christ, and sixteen million people joined a church. Yet only six million of those sixteen million actually attended a SBC church on any given Sunday.[2] That is ten million people unaccounted for.

Now, there may be good explanations for many of those individuals. Perhaps some of them joined a non-SBC church and forgot to tell their old congregation. But even accounting for mitigating factors, the reality is staggering: millions of people who once professed allegiance to Christ now have nothing to do with him. And that's just the SBC.

An Ancient Problem

Apostates and backsliders might be plentiful these days, but they're hardly new. The New Testament points to plenty of prominent people jumping ship in the early days of the church:

- *Judas Iscariot*—He was the granddaddy of them all. He looked like a true disciple of Christ (John 13:21–22). But in the end, he betrayed Jesus and killed himself (Matt. 27:5).
- *Hymenaeus, Alexander, and Philetus*—These men abandoned the truth of the gospel, shipwrecked their faith, and swerved from the truth (1 Tim. 1:19–20; 2 Tim. 2:17–18).
- *Demas*—Paul passes on Demas's friendly greeting to the churches in several of his letters. He must have been a close associate of the Apostle. But by the time Paul wrote his last letter, Demas had deserted him because of his love for the world (2 Tim. 4:10).

Scholars also think that the apostle John wrote his first letter in response to believers abandoning the faith. A group of professing Christians began to reject that Jesus, the Son of God, came in human flesh. This group broke away from the faithful congregation, leaving the remaining members confused, conflicted, and vulnerable.[3] John wanted to help the church understand this secession, so he told them, "They went out from us, but they were not of us; for if they had been of us, they would have continued with us. But they went out, that it might become plain that they all are not of us" (1 John 2:19). The departing members might have seemed like strong believers. Some of them might have been leaders in the congregation. But their true colors were now showing.

It's important to note what John was *not* saying. He was not saying, "These people were once Christians but no longer are." Rather, he was saying they were never Christians in the first place. They were never really "of us." Otherwise, they would still be in the church. The fact that they abandoned the faith demonstrates that they were never genuine believers.

Here's the underlying lesson as crisply as I can state it: the Bible teaches us that genuine Christians will not leave the faith. Genuine Christians don't abandon Christ.

What does that mean for your life and mine? It means that what matters is not whether we *once* acted and spoke like believers, but whether we're following Christ *today* and whether we continue doing so until the end.

Many American churches teach that being a Christian is just a matter of making a decision. If at some point in your life you want to be a Christian, tell God that you accept his forgiveness, and then the deal is done. They treat it like a measles vaccination, where you get a dose of forgiveness that permanently inoculates you against the fires of hell, whether you continue to follow Christ.

If that is the understanding of salvation that you had when you picked up this book, this chapter might seem radical. But let me assure you, it's not as radical as it sounds. In fact, many Christians in the past have treated these ideas as basic. For instance, the New Hampshire Baptist Confession of Faith, written in 1833, summarizes the Bible's teaching on this issue like this: "We believe that such only are real believers as endure unto the end; (and) that their persevering attachment to Christ is the grand mark which distinguishes them from superficial professors. . . ."[4]

How can we know who the real believers are? How can we distinguish them from those with superficial professions of faith? Real believers endure until the end. Their attachment to Christ perseveres and never goes away.

Right at the Heart of the Gospel

Notice that there are two errors to avoid here. On the one hand, we need to guard against the error of saying you can lose your salvation. A genuine Christian cannot. A genuine Christian *perseveres*. On the other hand, we need to guard against the error of those who flippantly use the words "Once saved, always saved!" as if you can make a decision for Christ but live like the Devil. That doesn't work, either. A genuine Christian perseveres *in following Christ*.

To see this, consider the nature of the salvation which Jesus secured for his people. It's far more than a "Get out of Hell Free" card. Rather:

- We were slaves to sin; Jesus came to set us free (Rom. 6:22).
- We were dead; Jesus came to give us life (Eph. 2:5).
- We were lost; Jesus came to seek us out (Luke 19:10).
- We were spiritually sick; Jesus came to heal us (Luke 5:31–32).
- We were spiritually blind; Jesus came so that we might see the truth (2 Cor. 4:4–6).
- We were rebellious children; Jesus came to restore us to our father (Luke 15:11–32).
- We were God's enemies; Jesus came to make us his friends (2 Cor. 5:18–19).
- We worshiped idols that could not help us; Jesus came to deliver us from their grip (1 Thess. 1:9).

Can you see why a true believer, who has genuinely experienced Christ's forgiveness, will remain in the faith until the end? From a human perspective, to be saved means to be saved from a life of disobedience and rebellion. Someone who continues to disobey and rebel simply has not been saved, because salvation, among other things, is salvation from *that*. It's like pointing to someone sitting in a puddle of mud and saying that you saved them from the mud. Your words make no sense. When someone who once professed faith now has no desire to worship, enjoy, obey, and love God, it demonstrates that he or she did not receive Jesus's reconciling, purifying salvation in the first place.

From Jesus's perspective, it's worth considering the metaphors for salvation. Someone who has been given sight cannot begin to *unsee*. Someone who has been raised to life is alive, not dead. Someone who has been adopted as a son is a son. The point is that Jesus saves. He doesn't save and then unsave. If he saved and then unsaved, he would not be a very good savior.

Reasons Why People Fall Away

Jesus once told a parable to help us understand why people might initially look like followers of Christ but eventually fall away. He said,

> "Listen! A sower went out to sow. And as he sowed, some seed fell along the path, and the birds came and devoured it. Other seed fell on rocky ground, where it did not have much soil, and immediately it sprang up, since it had no depth of soil. And when the sun rose, it was scorched, and since it had no root, it withered away. Other seed fell among thorns, and the thorns grew up and choked it, and it yielded no grain. And other seeds fell into good soil and produced grain, growing up and increasing and yielding thirtyfold and sixtyfold and a hundredfold." And he said, "He who has ears to hear, let him hear." (Mark 4:3–9)

Later on in that same chapter, Jesus explained the point of his story to his disciples. He told them that the four soils represented four different kinds of people and their different responses to God's Word:

> *The first category* of people hears God's Word and has no interest in it. Nothing happens because Satan lets nothing happen: "When they hear, Satan immediately comes and takes away the word that is sown in them" (Mark 4:15).
> *The second category* hears the Word of God and initially seems to accept it. They seem like Christians, but it doesn't last: "When tribulation or persecution arises on account of the word, immediately they fall away" (Mark 4:16–17).
> *The third category* of people hears the Word, but whatever positive response springs up, again, does not last: "The cares of the world and the deceitfulness of riches and the desires for other

things enter in and choke the word, and it proves unfruitful"
(Mark 4:18–19).

The final category of people hears the Word, and it sticks. It
saves. The growth springs up and endures: they "hear the word
and accept it and bear fruit, thirtyfold and sixtyfold and a hun-
dredfold" (Mark 4:20).

For our purposes, we're interested in the experiences of the
second and third categories of people in Jesus's parable. The
first wouldn't claim to be Christians, and the fourth persevere
in the faith and bear much fruit. But the second and third
both show initial signs of Christian commitment but do not
ultimately bear fruit and find salvation. By considering their
cases, we'll find two common reasons why people fall away
from the faith.

Persecution on Account of the Word

People in the second category hear the good news about
Jesus and receive it with joy. They are excited about Jesus
and enjoy the company of new Christian friends. Maybe they
are baptized, join the church, and begin to wear Christian
T-shirts.

But then persecution sets in. Maybe it's subtle—their fami-
lies and old friends make fun of their T-shirts. Maybe it's violent—the government threatens to throw them in jail or worse.
Whatever it is, they begin to pay a price for their association
with Jesus, just as Jesus promised them they would: "If they
persecuted me, they will also persecute you" (John 15:20).
Apparently, there is no way to follow after a Messiah who was
crucified by the world's powers that doesn't involve suffering.
And, sadly, Christians often fail to encourage people to "count
the cost" before deciding to follow Jesus.

Whether or not the members of this second group were
told to count the cost (please do when you share the gos-

pel!) the idea of following Jesus quickly loses its gleam under adverse circumstances. And there comes a point when it feels like more trouble than it's worth. Slowly but surely, these fair-weather followers distance themselves from the Christian community. Eventually, what they begin to call their "Christian phase" is a distant memory.

Compare this to the response of the people to whom the book of Hebrews was written. That church had been ostracized and was enduring persecution from government officials. The author of Hebrews, therefore, reminds these Christians of past suffering, celebrates their endurance, and encourages them to endure. He writes,

> But recall the former days when, after you were enlightened, you endured a hard struggle with sufferings, sometimes being publicly exposed to reproach and affliction, and sometimes being partners with those so treated. For you had compassion on those in prison, and you joyfully accepted the plundering of your property, since you knew that you yourselves had a better possession and an abiding one. Therefore do not throw away your confidence, which has a great reward. For you have need of endurance, so that when you have done the will of God you may receive what is promised. For, "Yet a little while, and the coming one will come and will not delay; but my righteous one shall live by faith, and if he shrinks back, my soul has no plea-sure in him." But we are not of those who shrink back and are destroyed, but of those who have faith and preserve their souls. (Heb. 10:32–39)

These true Christians endured persecution for the sake of Christ. They were publicly humiliated and financially ruined, but they clung tightly to Jesus and did not turn back. Like all believers throughout time, they had experienced the new birth and pledged their fealty to Jesus. No amount of trouble could pry them loose. Conversely, those who profess faith in Christ but then abandon him when trials hit were probably never genuinely Christians in the first place.

Prosperity That Chokes the Word

Members of the third category, like those in the second category, also receive the Word but eventually walk away from it. What distracts them is the cares of the world, whether that means they're poor and weighed down with anxiety over paying the rent, or they're rich and always looking for bigger and better homes.

The faith of some people is waylaid by poverty and suffering. The faith of others is choked out by too much success. Deprivation tempts some to abandon Christ for the hope of greener pastures. Prosperity causes others to lose sight of him. In other words, it's not about how much you have. It's about what you're after.

Now, we think of prosperity as a good thing, and in some ways it is. But it can be spiritually dangerous. Think about it:

- Material possessions can serve as an anesthetic, easing the soul's pain and numbing people to their need for Christ.
- Wealth tempts us to trust in it for our well-being rather than in Jesus.
- Prosperity means that we have more to lose, making it harder to leave everything for the sake of Christ.
- Riches are hard to come by. It requires much work and investment to gain and maintain wealth, leaving less time to devote to spiritual matters. As The Notorious B.I.G. put it: "Mo money, mo problems."
- And the more we own, the more we have potentially to treasure instead of Christ.

The Bible speaks repeatedly about the dangers of wealth. We will think about this more in a few chapters, but suffice it to say that someone who abandons Jesus in order to pursue wealth and prosperity never made him their treasure (Matt. 13:44–46).

Two Sides of a Coin

How then do we persevere in the faith and remain faithful until we die or Jesus returns (whichever comes first)? The book of Jude helps us answer that question. Jude writes,

> Keep yourselves in the love of God, waiting for the mercy of our Lord Jesus Christ that leads to eternal life. And have mercy on those who doubt; save others by snatching them out of the fire; to others show mercy with fear, hating even the garment stained by the flesh.
>
> Now to him who is able to keep you from stumbling and to present you blameless before the presence of his glory with great joy, to the only God, our Savior, through Jesus Christ our Lord, be glory, majesty, dominion, and authority, before all time and now and forever. Amen. (Jude 21–25)

Jude mentions two realities that we must keep in tension.

Perseverance Is a Believer's Responsibility

On one hand, Jude instructs us to keep ourselves "in the love of God." God loves us, yes, but we must keep ourselves in that love. In other words, perseverance is a believer's responsibility.

And Jude is not the only writer of the New Testament who talks this way. Throughout the New Testament, authors warn us to invest time and energy into making sure that we endure. They point to the constant danger of falling away precisely so that we will heed the warning and do what's necessary to remain faithful. Here are a few examples:

> And now, little children, abide in him, so that when he appears we may have confidence and not shrink from him in shame at his coming. (1 John 2:28)

> Fight the good fight of the faith. Take hold of the eternal life to which you were called and about which you made the good confession in the presence of many witnesses. I charge you in the presence of God, who gives life to all things, and of Christ Jesus, who in his testimony before Pontius Pilate made the good confession, to keep the commandment unstained and free from reproach until the appearing of our Lord Jesus Christ. (1 Tim. 6:12–14)

> Therefore do not throw away your confidence, which has a great reward. For you have need of endurance, so that when you have done the will of God you may receive what is promised. For, "Yet a little while, and the coming one will come and will not delay; but my righteous one shall live by faith, and if he shrinks back, my soul has no pleasure in him." But we are not of those who shrink back and are destroyed, but of those who have faith and preserve their souls. (Heb. 10:35–39)

> Therefore, since we are surrounded by so great a cloud of witnesses, let us also lay aside every weight, and sin which clings so closely, and let us run with endurance the race that is set before us. (Heb. 12:1)

These warnings and exhortations assume that perseverance is the work and responsibility of every individual Christian.

In short, there is a difference between my wife and me when it comes to running. She endures; I do not. So it is in the Christian life: we're called to endure. In Jesus's words, one more time, "But the one who endures to the end will be saved" (Matt. 10:22).

Perseverance Is God's Work

On the other hand, this is only half of the picture. If the only thing you remember from this chapter is the opening illustration about my wife's perseverance, you will have missed something crucial. We must persevere, yes, but perseverance is ultimately God's work.

Jude did not put his confidence finally in his readers' hard work or effort. He also reminded them that God "is able to keep you from stumbling and to present you blameless before the presence of his glory with great joy" (Jude 24).

Believers can have confidence that they will endure until the end because it's the Lord himself who keeps his people faithful. God uses the warnings of Scripture listed above to alert his people and to empower them to avoid falling away. Listen once more:

> And I am sure of this, that he who began a good work in you will bring it to completion at the day of Jesus Christ. (Phil. 1:6)
>
> In him you also, when you heard the word of truth, the gospel of your salvation, and believed in him, were sealed with the promised Holy Spirit, who is the guarantee of our inheritance until we acquire possession of it, to the praise of his glory. (Eph. 1:13–14)
>
> My sheep hear my voice, and I know them, and they follow me. I give them eternal life, and they will never perish, and no one will snatch them out of my hand. My Father, who has given them to me, is greater than all, and no one is able to snatch them out of the Father's hand. (John 10:27–29)
>
> For I am sure that neither death nor life, nor angels nor rulers, nor things present nor things to come, nor powers, nor height nor depth, nor anything else in all creation, will be able to separate us from the love of God in Christ Jesus our Lord. (Rom. 8:38–39)

Just as believers' salvation is not their own doing, neither is their perseverance. The amazing grace which saves wretches is the same amazing grace that brings them home.

Does Jesus's promise that no one can snatch us from his hand, or God's promise that nothing can separate us from the love of Christ, mean that we can sit back and do nothing? Not at all. We work, knowing that God works through us. Here's how

Paul puts both sides of the coin together in one verse: "Work out your own salvation with fear and trembling, for it is God who works in you, both to will and to work for his good pleasure" (Phil. 2:12–13).

Conclusion

If you are currently walking with Christ, this chapter is not intended to frighten you. You can have confidence that the Lord will keep close to you as you follow him. Continue to fight the good fight and endure until the final buzzer sounds. Devote yourself to encouraging other Christians to do the same.

If, however, you have fallen away from the faith, or you are considering leaving the faith, heed this warning! If you are relying on some past profession of faith that has nothing to do with your day-to-day life, I pray that you will hear Scripture calling you to come to Christ. If you have walked away from Christ, you are not a Christian.

How to Respond

Reflect:

Why does the nature of Christ's salvation mean that a true believer will not return to a life of unbelief?

Are you following Christ right now?

How can perseverance be both our responsibility and God's responsibility?

Repent:

Confess to God the ways that the world has conspired with your own sinful desires to tempt you to stop following Jesus. Ask him to forgive you for your fickle faith.

Remember:

> Meditate on the words of Psalm 130:3–4: "If you, O LORD, should mark iniquities, O Lord, who could stand? But with you there is forgiveness, that you may be feared."

> Thank God that he does not mark our iniquities, but he laid them all on his Son so that we might be forgiven. We cannot work hard enough to keep ourselves in the faith, so praise him that he holds his sheep in the palm of his hand.

Report:

> What is the role of the local church in helping God's people endure in the faith?

> Do you have someone in your life who is encouraging you to stay faithful to Christ? If not, who could serve that role for you?

6

You Are Not a Christian
If You Don't Love Other People

FOR 99 PERCENT OF US, growing up means learning to accept our limitations. When I was young, I wanted to be a doctor, a fireman, and a professional baseball player. As I got older, I discovered that time was limited and that I would have to start with just being a baseball player. Being a doctor and a fireman could wait until the sports career was over.

Still a little later, maybe when I was eleven, each of these dreams began to fall apart. I was slow of foot. My lack of hand-eye coordination meant that I was never going to hit a curveball regularly. The sight of blood repelled me. And it became evident to me that it is in fact better to run out of burning buildings than to run into them. Little by little, the verdict was coming in: I wasn't going to be a baseball player, a doctor, or a fireman.

Several years of anxiety and hand wringing about the future followed. Then, sometime in late junior high, I realized what I should do with my life: I would be a college professor. A professional smart guy. Short of being the first baseman for the New York Yankees, what could be better? You are basically paid to read a lot of books, talk to students two days a week, and take the summers off. Throw in my penchant for wearing tweed and smoking a pipe, and it looked like a perfect fit. I would be a literature professor. My existential crisis was over. . . .

. . . until Charles Dickens came along. Have you ever read Dickens? His novels are the literary equivalent of wheat grass: beloved by a small group of devotees, doubtlessly good for you, but really hard to choke down. When my ninth-grade English teacher assigned Dickens's novel *Hard Times* to our class, I was at first excited. I knew that a person needed to appreciate Dickens in order to be a professional egghead. Here was my chance to take an exhilarating first step into a new destiny.

But by page six, all of my hopes were dashed, and panic had set in. *Hard Times* is a fictional criticism of utilitarianism, and it must be one of the most boring works of fiction ever written. Well, to be accurate, all I can say for sure is that the first six pages must be some of the most boring six pages of fiction ever written. After that, all I can say is that *Hard Times* begat the most boring CliffsNotes ever written. I remain convinced that no human being has successfully finished this novel; everyone is just pretending.

In fact, my distaste for Dickens lasted for years. I never read *Great Expectations*. I avoided *A Tale of Two Cities* like the plague. I even refused to watch the musical *Oliver!*, based on the Dickens novel *Oliver Twist*, when it was shown on television during the local PBS station's annual membership drive. If a man could write a book as boring as *Hard Times*, how excruciating would the musical version *Oliver!* be?

There was one exception to my distaste for Dickens. Every Christmas season, I watched some version of the movie *A Christmas Carol* (Alastair Sim, George C. Scott, Patrick Stewart, the Muppets), and I loved all of them. The story of Ebenezer Scrooge's transformation from curmudgeon to philanthropist is heartwarming, engaging, and relentlessly entertaining— everything *Hard Times* is not. Still, I could not bring myself to read the books on which the movies were based. The memories of ninth-grade boredom were too painful.

Well, on one fateful day, with the encouragement of my lovely wife, I faced my fears and cracked the spine of *A Christmas Carol*. At first I was scared, as if the words on the page would seep through my eyes like a boredom virus, pulling me into a dull torpor. But I was pleasantly surprised. The book was every bit as good as the movies, maybe even better. And despite the author's complete inability to make Thomas Gradgrind Jr. and the other characters in *Hard Times* even remotely interesting, his descriptions of Ebenezer Scrooge were delightful. Listen to this passage:

> Oh! But he was a tight-fisted hand at the grindstone, Scrooge! a squeezing, wrenching, grasping, scraping, clutching, covetous, old sinner! Hard and sharp as flint, from which no steel had ever struck out generous fire; secret, and self-contained, and solitary as an oyster. The cold within him froze his old features, nipped his pointed nose, shrivelled his cheek, stiffened his gait; made his eyes red, his thin lips blue; and spoke out shrewdly in his grating voice. A frosty rime was on his head, and on his eyebrows, and his wiry chin. He carried his own low temperature always about with him; he iced his office in the dog-days; and didn't thaw it one degree at Christmas.[1]

The depth of Scrooge's misanthropy makes his transformation all the more satisfying and delightful. By the time the story ends, we read:

> Scrooge was better than his word. He did it all, and infinitely more; and to Tiny Tim, who did not die, he was a second father. He became as good a friend, as good a master, and as good a man, as the good old city knew, or any other good old city, town, or borough, in the good old world. Some people laughed to see the alteration in him, but he let them laugh, and little

heeded them; for he was wise enough to know that nothing ever happened on this globe, for good, at which some people did not have their fill of laughter in the outset; and knowing that such as these would be blind anyway, he thought it quite as well that they should wrinkle up their eyes in grins, as have the malady in less attractive forms. His own heart laughed: and that was quite enough for him.[2]

Everyone loves a story of redemption and reclamation. That explains why *A Christmas Carol* is a perennial favorite.

Still, we all know that things like this do not happen in real life. Leopards don't change their spots. People don't learn to love after a lifetime of wickedness. The Ebenezer Scrooges of the world do not suddenly become Mother Theresas. Right?

Or do they? In some ways, the point of the book you are now holding is to say that it's exactly this kind of change that occurs among Christians. One of the most important changes that always accompanies true repentance and faith, says the Bible, is a growth in genuine love for other people. In fact, if this kind of change has not accompanied your conversion, there's reason to ask whether you are really a Christian.

I am not making this up. I'm getting it from the apostle John. Listen to him: "Beloved, let us love one another, for love is from God, and whoever loves has been born of God and knows God. *Anyone who does not love does not know God*, because God is love" (1 John 4:7–8). The point is pretty simple: you are not a Christian if you don't love people.

A Crazy Kind of Love

Admittedly, this is a tough statement—tough because it demands that we examine our hearts and lives honestly. But it's also tough because, well, it's hard to know how much love is expected. I mean, everyone loves something or somebody. Even the worst people I know love their friends or their moms or their kids. If you have to love in order to be a Christian, who *doesn't* meet that criterion?

Everyone loves love. If you stood up in a meeting of Christians, Muslims, Jews, Buddhists, and Hindus and said, "God is love," you would see a lot of nodding. People like the idea of a God who is love. They even like the idea of a religion that tells people to love. Think about it: Americans have a holiday solely devoted to expressing love.[3] Greeting cards sell by the millions. And at least two Jennifer Aniston romantic comedies are foisted on the population every year. But in a world where fuzzy notions of love sell, what does it mean to "have love" in a uniquely Christian way?

To answer this question, we need to dig deeper into what the Bible tells us about how Christians should love. The Bible tells us that Christians will be marked by three specific kinds of love. As we go, you'll find that I point to a lot of Scripture. Don't just skip over these passages. Read them. You don't want my opinions to reshape your understanding of love. You want the Bible to reshape it. Furthermore, I want to leave you without any thought that I'm pulling the wool over your eyes. What you find here is *basic Christianity*. If you can, pause a moment on each scriptural passage and meditate on it.

Love for Other Christians

On the night before he was crucified, Jesus gave his disciples a final instruction, a new commandment. He said to them, "A new commandment I give to you, that you love one another: just as I have loved you, you also are to love one another. By this all people will know that you are my disciples, if you have love for one another" (John 13:34–35). Jesus's disciples should love each other in ways that are extraordinary by the world's standards. It's one of the hallmarks and calling cards of Christ's followers.

This love normally manifests itself in the context of life in a local church. Members of a local church should care for one another physically and spiritually, as the New Testament writers instructed the earliest churches to do. For instance, the writer to the Hebrews tells the church to "let brotherly love continue," and to do so by remembering brothers and sisters in prison for their faith, by sharing what they had, and by making the leaders' service a joy (Heb. 13:1, 3, 17).

Peter, knowing how difficult it can be to love our fellow church members, writes, "Above all, keep loving one another earnestly, since love covers a multitude of sins" (1 Pet. 4:8). They're going to sin against you, but love them anyway! And you know what else? Exercise hospitality toward them, and don't grumble while you do (v. 9). Furthermore, you know a man is a leader when he can exercise this kind of love and care for a congregation (1 Pet. 5:2–3).

Time and time again, Scripture commands Christians to love each other.[4] So John tells us that love for other Christians is one of the hallmarks of a genuine disciple, and a lack of love is a sign of a false professor:

> Whoever says he is in the light and hates his brother is still in darkness. Whoever loves his brother abides in the light, and in him there is no cause for stumbling. But whoever hates his brother is in the darkness and walks in the darkness, and does not know where he is going, because the darkness has blinded his eyes. (1 John 2:9–11)

Love for Those in Need

Another characteristic of Christian love is that it tends toward the poor and needy. John's first letter, once again, challenges us right here. John pointedly asks, "But if anyone has the world's goods and sees his brother in need, yet closes his heart against him, how does God's love abide in him?" (1 John 3:17). There is no way to have God's love abiding in you without its overflowing in acts of mercy toward those in need. If we claim that we have faith in Christ but refuse to help someone in need, our faith is dead and useless (James 2:15–17).

It appears that this kind of love for the poor characterized the first Christians. Around AD 45, a famine broke out in Jerusalem that had a terrible impact on the Christians in the city. The churches of Macedonia, in response, gave generously to the relief effort, even though they themselves were quite poor. We also know that congregations had regular relief programs for poor widows (1 Tim. 5:3ff.), and that care for the poor was a hallmark of godliness in the early church (Acts 9:36ff., Acts 10:4).

This pattern of life impressed even hostile outsiders. In AD 197, Tertullian, an early church leader, wrote his *Apology* to defend Christians to the hostile Roman authorities. Tertullian described the extraordinary love that Christians showed to their brothers and sisters in need, a love so great that it brought scorn from their pagan neighbors. He wrote,

> Though we have our treasure-chest, it is not made up of purchase money, as of a religion that has its price. On the monthly collection day, if he likes, each puts in a small donation; but only if it be his pleasure, and only if he be able: for there is no compulsion; all is voluntary. These gifts . . . are not taken thence and spent on feasts, and drinking-bouts, and eating-houses, but to support and bury poor people, to supply the wants of boys and girls destitute of means and parents, and of old persons confined now to the house; such, too, as have suffered shipwreck; and if there happen to be any in the mines, or banished to the islands, or shut up in the prisons, for nothing but their fidelity to the cause of God's church, they become the nurslings of their confession. But it is mainly the deeds of a love so noble that lead many to put a brand upon us. *See*, they say, *how they love one*

another . . . how they are ready even to die for one another. (italics mine)[5]

Back in chapter 1, we briefly looked at Jesus's teaching in Matthew 25. If you remember, Jesus tells his hearers that he will one day return and separate his people (the sheep) from those who are not Christians (the goats). He then goes on to describe what particularly characterizes the sheep:

> Then the King will say to those on his right, "Come, you who are blessed by my Father, inherit the kingdom prepared for you from the foundation of the world. For I was hungry and you gave me food, I was thirsty and you gave me drink, I was a stranger and you welcomed me, I was naked and you clothed me, I was sick and you visited me, I was in prison and you came to me." Then the righteous will answer him, saying, "Lord, when did we see you hungry and feed you, or thirsty and give you drink? And when did we see you a stranger and welcome you, or naked and clothe you? And when did we see you sick or in prison and visit you?" And the King will answer them, "Truly, I say to you, as you did it to one of the least of these my brothers, you did it to me." (Matt. 25:34–40)

The goats on the other hand showed no such compassion for those in need. Jesus continues,

> Then he will say to those on his left, "Depart from me, you cursed, into the eternal fire prepared for the devil and his angels. For I was hungry and you gave me no food, I was thirsty and you gave me no drink, I was a stranger and you did not welcome me, naked and you did not clothe me, sick and in prison and you did not visit me." Then they also will answer, saying, "Lord, when did we see you hungry or thirsty or a stranger or naked or sick or in prison, and did not minister to you?" Then he will answer them, saying, "Truly, I say to you, as you did not do it to one of the least of these, you did not do it to me." And

these will go away into eternal punishment, but the righteous into eternal life. (Matt. 25:41–46)

I don't know how someone could more forcefully or harrowingly make this point. When King Jesus returns, he will be able to spot his people because of the love that they have showed to those in need.

Love for Your Enemies

The third type of love that characterizes a genuine Christian is love for one's enemies. This is perhaps the most difficult but most distinct form of love enjoined by Jesus. He observes that even the worst kinds of sinners love people who love them. But that's not enough for his people. He says,

> But I say to you who hear, Love your enemies, do good to those who hate you, bless those who curse you, pray for those who abuse you. To one who strikes you on the cheek, offer the other also, and from one who takes away your cloak do not withhold your tunic either. Give to everyone who begs from you, and from one who takes away your goods do not demand them back. And as you wish that others would do to you, do so to them.
>
> If you love those who love you, what benefit is that to you? For even sinners love those who love them. And if you do good to those who do good to you, what benefit is that to you? For even sinners do the same. And if you lend to those from whom you expect to receive, what credit is that to you? Even sinners lend to sinners, to get back the same amount. But love your enemies, and do good, and lend, expecting nothing in return, and your reward will be great, and you will be sons of the Most High, for he is kind to the ungrateful and the evil. Be merciful, even as your Father is merciful. (Luke 6:27–36)

A Christian should be marked by such counterintuitive, unnatural love. Everything in us naturally loves those who are kind to us and naturally hates those who oppose us. But everyone who has been born of God and who follows Jesus as Lord loves supernaturally, which means loving those who oppose us.

What's Love God to Do With It?

True Christians love. They love other Christians, the needy, and their enemies. Why do they love like this? Remember what 1 John 4:7 says: Christians have been born of God, and God is love. Christians love like this because, by the power of the Spirit, they reflect the character of God himself. Look closely at the reasons that Scripture gives for why this love must be present.

> Anyone who does not love does not know God, *because God is love*. (1 John 4:8)
>
> A new commandment I give to you, that you love one another: *just as I have loved you*, you also are to love one another. (John 13:34)
>
> But I say to you, Love your enemies and pray for those who persecute you, so that you may be sons of your Father who is in heaven. *For he makes his sun rise on the evil and on the good*, and sends rain on the just and on the unjust. (Matt. 5:44–45)

In each one of these verses, Christians are commanded to love because God himself loves. Our love shows that God's love is in us, and it demonstrates what he is like. We love other Christians, the needy, and our enemies because those are the people that God loves.

God Loves His People—Christians

God's love for his people is a marvelous thing. In fact, the entire Christian message displays the glories of God's gracious, undeserved love for the people he saves. God repeatedly reminds Christians that their salvation displays his love for them.

But God, being rich in mercy, *because of the great love with which he loved us*, even when we were dead in our trespasses, made us alive together with Christ—by grace you have been saved. (Eph. 2:4–5)

... that you, being rooted and grounded in love, may have strength to comprehend with all the saints *what is the breadth and length and height and depth, and to know the love of Christ that surpasses knowledge.* (Eph. 3:17–19)

But when *the goodness and loving kindness of God our Savior* appeared, he saved us, not because of works done by us in righteousness, but according to his own mercy, by the washing of regeneration and renewal of the Holy Spirit. (Titus 3:4–5)

See *what kind of love* the Father has given to us, that we should be called children of God; and so we are. (1 John 3:1)

Why has God saved his people? Why has he made them his children? It's not because of anything in them. Rather, it's entirely a matter of God's amazing love. He loves his people, and so he sent his Son to save them.

God Loves Those in Need

We naturally love people who are successful, wealthy, and put together. If you were at a party and a famous athlete or Hollywood star walked in, you would spend the rest of the evening talking about it. But God declares that he sets his love on the needy, the poor, the widows, the orphans, and those who cry to him for help.

For the LORD your God is God of gods and Lord of lords, the great, the mighty, and the awesome God, who is not partial and takes no bribe. *He executes justice for the fatherless and the widow, and loves the sojourner*, giving him food and clothing. Love the sojourner, therefore.... (Deut. 10:17–19)

Listen, my beloved brothers, has not God chosen those who are poor in the world to be rich in faith and heirs of the kingdom, which he has promised to those who love him? (James 2:5)

And he lifted up his eyes on his disciples, and said: "Blessed are you who are poor, for yours is the kingdom of God. Blessed are you who are hungry now, for you shall be satisfied. Blessed are you who weep now, for you shall laugh." (Luke 6:20–21)

In an unexpected reversal of fortune, the poor and needy have the spiritual inside track on the rich and powerful. Fame and pleasure have a way of numbing people to their need for God. But desperate people are more likely to cry out to God and thus find him merciful and willing to help.

God Loves His Enemies

It's one thing for God to love people who give him no reason to love them. It's another thing for him to love the poor and needy who can't pay him back. But it's absolutely flabbergasting that a holy and just God would love his enemies instead of crushing them.

Yet it is one expression of God's perfection that he loves like this. Listen to a final set of passages:

For *he makes his sun rise on the evil* and on the good, and sends rain on the just and on the unjust. For if you love those who love you, what reward do you have? Do not even the tax collectors do the same? And if you greet only your brothers, what more are you doing than others? Do not even the Gentiles do the same? You therefore must be perfect, as your heavenly Father is perfect. (Matt. 5:45–48)

And when they came to the place that is called The Skull, there they crucified him, and the criminals, one on his right and one on his left. And Jesus said, "Father, *forgive them, for they know not what they do.*" (Luke 23:33–34)

But *God shows his love for us* in that while we were still sinners, Christ died for us. Since, therefore, we have now been justified by his blood, much more shall we be saved by him from the wrath of God. For if *while we were enemies* we were reconciled to God by the death of his Son, much more, now that we are reconciled, shall we be saved by his life. (Rom. 5:8–10)

Where's the Love?

In chapter 4 we considered how our attitude toward sin reveals the identity of our father. If we love sin, Satan must be our father. If we love righteousness, God must be our father.

In the same way, the manner in which you love shows to whom you belong. If you only love those who love you, you are not followers of Jesus. Remember, Jesus forgave his tormentors. If God himself showed such costly love to his people—even the annoying, lame, and needy ones—so will his followers. God is love. And so does everyone born of God.

How to Respond

Reflect:

> What does Christian love look like? How is that love rooted in the love that God has for people?
>
> Where in your life do you see evidence of that kind of love?
>
> Can people who are not Christians show genuine love? If so, how is it different from the love a Christian has?

Repent:

> Confess to God the ways in which selfishness, jealousy, and pride have kept you from being loving. Ask him to forgive you for all of the ways in which you could have shown love but chose not to.
>
> Think of one person to whom you could show love in the coming weeks. Make a plan to do so.

Remember:

Read Romans 5:8: "God shows his love for us in that while we were still sinners, Christ died for us."

Take time to remember how marvelously God has loved us by sending his Son. We cannot love others enough to earn that love. Instead, understanding God's love for us despite our sin enables us with love for other people.

Report:

Ask someone in your church to help you evaluate whether your life is marked by love.

How does being involved in a local church help you grow in the kinds of love discussed in this chapter?

7

You Are Not a Christian
If You Love Your Stuff

HAVING ARMS IS GREAT. You might take them for granted, but think of all the things that you do with your arms:

- Get dressed in the morning
- Brush your teeth
- Hug your family
- Put your fare card in the turnstile to get on the subway
- Eat your lunch
- Turn the pages of a book so that you can read the rest of a brilliant, attention-arresting chapter introduction

All day, every day you use your arms. You depend on them. You could probably get by with just one arm. You could even survive life with none. But let's face it—you wouldn't want to do either.

And mountain climber Aron Ralston would probably agree with you. But Ralston also knows that some things are even more precious than an arm. On a cold day in April 2003, Ralston was hiking by himself in Blue John Canyon in the remote deserts of Utah. Ralston was an experienced hiker, having climbed most of the 14,000-foot mountains in the Rockies. Ralston had also experienced his share of danger. Two months earlier he had been buried up to his neck in snow by an avalanche in Colorado. He managed to dig himself out and save a companion who was wholly buried.

But on this Saturday in April, Ralston hiked through a 3-foot wide slot in the gorge only to have a 900-pound boulder fall and pin his arm to the canyon wall. He struggled to free his arm, but to no avail. A long hard night followed. Sometime the next day, he realized that calling for help was useless. On Tuesday he ran out of water. On Thursday, he realized that he was going to die if he didn't take drastic measures.

At this point, squeamish readers should skip ahead. What comes next is not for the faint of heart. Using his one free arm and his teeth, Ralston fashioned a tourniquet out of backpack straps. Twisting his body violently, he cracked the radius and ulna bones in his arm. He then used a dull penknife to cut bit by bit through the skin, muscles, and nerves of his arm. Finally, he used his multi-tool's pliers to tear the tenacious arm tendons. The entire operation took about an hour.

Ralston left his arm pinned to the canyon wall, rappelled down a 65-foot cliff, and climbed out of the gorge where he was rescued by a group of hikers. He now lives in Colorado and continues to climb mountains.

There are a lot of lessons to be learned from his story, not the least of which is the folly of hiking in remote desert canyons by yourself. And he certainly has a ready-made illustration if he ever finds himself in a pulpit preaching Jesus's words about cutting off your hand if it causes you to sin.

Yet here's the moral I want to take from Ralston's story: there are times when wisdom calls us to sacrifice something extremely valuable, even if it might otherwise be a good thing. Ralston, no doubt, made the correct choice. Arms are great, but they are not more valuable than life itself. There are times when losing is gaining. And we surely want to give up something we cannot keep, to borrow from Jim Elliot, in order to gain something ultimately valuable.

Like arms, money and material possessions are also good things. They are gifts from God to be enjoyed. In a certain respect, we can even say they are necessary for living in this world. What many people who call themselves Christians do not realize, however, is how easily all our stuff—or dreams of stuff—keeps us pinned to the wall and threatens to take our soul. In fact, let me put it like this: you are not a Christian if you love your stuff.

A Painful Choice

In Luke's Gospel we read about another young man who was pinned to the wall. But it wasn't a boulder that kept him fastened; it was his wealth. The problem was that he didn't know it.

The story begins when the young man, who was a ruler, approached Jesus with a question:

> And a ruler asked him, "Good Teacher, what must I do to inherit eternal life?" And Jesus said to him, ". . . You know the commandments: 'Do not commit adultery, Do not murder, Do not steal, Do not bear false witness, Honor your father and mother.'" And he said, "All these I have kept from my youth." (Luke 18:18–21)

The man wanted to know what he must do in order to inherit eternal life. We cannot know whether this was an honest question. Obviously, he was satisfied with his religious performance. There was no adultery or lying or stealing or murder on the permanent record. So either he was looking for a pat on the back from the famous teacher, or he was anxiously trying to make sure he had covered all his bases. The point is, on the outside, this man was as good as you or me, and probably better. Count up all the good things you've done and all the times you have obeyed God's law, and then double it. That's probably this guy.

Now, consider how Jesus responds:

> When Jesus heard this, he said to him, "One thing you still lack. Sell all that you have and distribute to the poor, and you will have treasure in heaven; and come, follow me." But when he heard these things, he became very sad, for he was extremely rich. Jesus, seeing that he had become sad, said, "How difficult it is for those who have wealth to enter the kingdom of God! For it is easier for a camel to go through the eye of a needle than for a rich person to enter the kingdom of God." (Luke 18:22–25)

That is not what we expect Jesus to say. We expect that Jesus would either affirm him ("Wow, you really are holy! Good job!") or correct him ("Wait a minute, big guy. Remember that lie you told back in January?"). But Jesus ignores the man's external conformity and focuses instead on his heart.

It turns out this man lacked one thing. He had a lot of treasure here on earth. He was rich—not upper-middle class, not well off, but "extremely rich." Understandably, he loved his money. But Jesus said that if this rich ruler wanted treasure in heaven—that is, salvation—his stuff had to go. He could not have both his wealth and the kingdom of God. Why not?

Money Is a Blessing

Before answering that question, let's make sure we understand what Jesus is *not* saying here. He is not telling this rich man that all money is inherently evil. In fact, money and prosperity honestly acquired can be a great blessing from God. Consider four things that the Bible tells us about wealth.

1) God created the earth to be prosperous.

> God blessed [Adam and Eve]. And God said to them, "Be fruit-ful and multiply and fill the earth and subdue it and have dominion over the fish of the sea and over the birds of the heavens and over every living thing that moves on the earth." And God said, "Behold, I have given you every plant yielding seed that is on the face of all the earth, and every tree with seed in its fruit. You shall have them for food. And to every beast of the earth and to every bird of the heavens and to everything that creeps on the earth, everything that has the breath of life, I have given every green plant for food." And it was so. And God saw everything that he had made, and be-hold, it was very good. (Gen. 1:28–31)

2) Prosperity is oftentimes the fruit of obedience and wisdom.

> And because you listen to these rules and keep and do them, the LORD your God . . . will also bless the fruit of your womb and the fruit of your ground, your grain and your wine and your oil, the increase of your herds and the young of your flock, in the land that he swore to your fathers to give you. . . . There shall not be male or female barren among you or among your live-stock. (Deut. 7:12–14)
>
> You shall remember the LORD your God, for it is he who gives you power to get wealth, that he may confirm his covenant that he swore to your fathers, as it is this day. (Deut. 8:18)
>
> The blessing of the LORD makes rich, and he adds no sor-row with it. (Prov. 10:22)
>
> Whoever is slothful will not roast his game, but the dili-gent man will get precious wealth. (Prov. 12:27)
>
> The crown of the wise is their wealth, but the folly of fools brings folly. (Prov. 14:24)

3) Wealth helps us provide for the needy.

> Whoever gives to the poor will not want, but he who hides his eyes will get many a curse (Prov. 28:27).

> And he [John the Baptist] answered them, "Whoever has two tunics is to share with him who has none, and whoever has food is to do likewise." (Luke 3:11)

4) *When Jesus returns and makes all things new, God's people will again be prosperous.*

> Then the angel showed me the river of the water of life, bright as crystal, flowing from the throne of God and of the Lamb through the middle of the street of the city; also, on either side of the river, the tree of life with its twelve kinds of fruit, yielding its fruit each month. The leaves of the tree were for the healing of the nations. No longer will there be anything accursed, but the throne of God and of the Lamb will be in it, and his servants will worship him. (Rev. 22:1–3)

We all intuitively understand that money can be a good thing. When your kids are sick, it's a blessing to have money to pay for their care. When you're hungry, it's good to have money to fill your stomach. If this book came with a crisp $100 bill tucked inside the cover, you would not recoil in horror; you would buy more copies of this book and give them to friends. So Jesus is not telling this rich young ruler that his wealth is inherently sinful. Money is a blessing from God for which we should be thankful.

Money Is Dangerous

But don't change the station yet. There's more to say about money that's of life-and-death importance. In a fallen world, money and possessions are inherently dangerous. The rich young man was blind to this fact.

Money can make life easier. It has the power to give us what we want. Therefore, human beings are constantly tempted to make an idol out of their wealth. Instead of trusting God's power and goodness, we trust money's power and our own goodness. We trust it for happiness and security. Instead of

looking to God for satisfaction, we grow attached to our possessions and look to them for meaning and satisfaction. If
you don't believe me, just consider the hysteria which fills the
newspapers when the stock market crashes or housing values
plummet.

So dangerous is money that Jesus warned his disciples
that rich people will have an extremely hard time getting into
the kingdom of God. More money means more temptation to
abandon God and trust wealth. In Luke 12, Jesus tells a parable
that illustrates this point:

> And he said to them, "Take care, and be on your guard against
> all covetousness, for one's life does not consist in the abun-
> dance of his possessions." And he told them a parable, saying,
> "The land of a rich man produced plentifully, and he thought
> to himself, 'What shall I do, for I have nowhere to store my
> crops?' And he said, 'I will do this: I will tear down my barns
> and build larger ones, and there I will store all my grain and my
> goods. And I will say to my soul, Soul, you have ample goods
> laid up for many years; relax, eat, drink, be merry.' But God said
> to him, 'Fool! This night your soul is required of you, and the
> things you have prepared, whose will they be?' So is the one
> who lays up treasure for himself and is not rich toward God."
> (Luke 12:15–21)

In Jesus's story a rich man has a field that produces a great
crop, which will make him even richer. And so he makes a
shrewd financial decision: he invests in his infrastructure
by building a bigger barn. Now he has everything: a comfortable retirement, a nice nest egg, a little rest from worry and
stress. Eat, drink, and be merry . . . that sounds pretty good,
doesn't it?

But there's a catch. He dies. God demands his life. It turns
out that barns filled with wheat are not very useful when
God's judgment comes. The man may have been a shrewd

businessman, but the shrewd businessman was finally a fool. He spent his life pursuing the wrong kind of riches. When it came time for him to give an account for his life, he was not prepared. Proverbs 11:4 drives the point home bluntly: "Riches do not profit in the day of wrath, but righteousness delivers from death."

Wealth is like anesthesia: it can be a great thing, but it can also be dangerous. If you have a life-threatening wound, you don't want to be so numbed on anesthesia that you don't recognize the danger. Anesthesia does not fix your problems; it does not heal your wounds. It just makes you less aware of the problems that you have.

All your wealth is dangerous because it has the power to numb you to your need for God. It has the power to draw your love away from God and deceive you into thinking it can satisfy and save you. The apostle Paul concludes bluntly, "For the love of money is a root of all kinds of evils" (1 Tim. 6:10).

Two Lords, One Choice

So dangerous is the love of money, in fact, that Jesus described it as one of the chief pretenders to God's throne. He knew that it presents itself as a would-be savior, offering salvation through comfort and ease. So he warned his listeners in the starkest terms: "No servant can serve two masters, for either he will hate the one and love the other, or he will be devoted to the one and despise the other. You cannot serve God and money" (Luke 16:13).

Think about it. There are two gods making a claim on your life. One of them is the true God of the universe, who is ready to help and to save. You will find freedom, joy, and eternal life serving him. The other god is, in fact, no god at all, but that doesn't stop it from making promises it cannot keep. In fact, this other god will require more and more time, more and more anxiety, and more and more love and energy, but it will never provide the ultimate payoff of joy and peace. This god is a slave master who lies. So which god do you want to serve?

If you come to Christ, you cannot do so halfheartedly. Jesus won't share your affections or your heart with anything else. This is not because he's petty or doesn't play nice. It's because he is kind, and he knows these other things are killing you. They have you pinned to the canyon wall whether you realize it or not.

Nothing else can deliver what you need. Your money, job, success, kids, spouse, hopes, ambitions, dreams, reputation . . . all of them may be good things. But none of them can meet your greatest needs. Our hearts are bent to think they can. We look at those things and think, "That will save me and give me joy, purpose, and meaning." But if you try to find joy in anything other than Jesus, it will end badly.

Jesus confronts us and offers to untangle us from our covetousness and enslaving idolatry. Most of us don't own our stuff; our stuff owns us. So Jesus comes to set us free. Graciously, he exposes our false loves. He shows us that our hearts are idolatrous, and he extends his gracious salvation to anyone who will enter his service.

The radical nature of discipleship forces a choice. Jesus says we cannot serve God and money because he will admit no rivals. His salvation demands total commitment. You cannot be a Christian if pursuing riches on earth is the organizing principle of your life. Instead, you must be willing to sacrifice everything in order to have Jesus as your Lord.

In Matthew 13, Jesus tells two brief parables to help illustrate this truth:

> The kingdom of heaven is like treasure hidden in a field, which a man found and covered up. Then in his joy he goes and sells all that he has and buys that field. Again, the kingdom of

heaven is like a merchant in search of fine pearls, who, on finding one pearl of great value, went and sold all that he had and
bought it. (Matt. 13:44–46)

Each of these men made the discovery of a lifetime. The first
man found a treasure in a field; the second found the most
magnificent pearl. That is what the kingdom of heaven is
like. The salvation Jesus offers is a treasure of unsurpassed
value.

In order to obtain this treasure, both men had to sell every
other possession they owned. The pearl merchant would have
been a rich man, so this was no small sacrifice. Presumably,
finding the treasure produced a moment of crisis for both.
They could not have this treasure and hold onto everything
they loved and had worked for. They had to forsake it all.
The kingdom of heaven must be obtained in the same way. It
requires us to cash in all of our chips. It can only be obtained
at the cost of everything.

In the same way, there is a choice before all of us, a choice
about whom we will serve and invest our lives in. Will we
serve God or our money and possessions? Maybe it sounds
like an obvious choice. But billions of people choose poorly
every day.

There is in fact a great danger of failing to heed Jesus here.
The rich young ruler did. He had everything you and I probably
want in life. He was rich, powerful, and unimpeachable in personal conduct. But he left Jesus's presence that day as the slave
of a worthless idol. Given a stark choice between following
Jesus or his money, he chose the money. He missed the salvation right in front of him and walked away as an outwardly
moral man with no hope.

Does Jesus call everyone to literally sell everything and
give away their money? No, but he does call everyone to love
and trust him more than money, and one of the best ways to

reveal whether we do is to consider the challenge of giving more away. If you ultimately love and trust your stuff, if you choose to serve your money for your own purposes, you are not a follower of Christ.

What It Means to Follow Jesus

Following after Jesus requires us to pay a price. We cannot serve Jesus and our money, so when the demands of the two come into conflict, we see whom we really serve. We must be willing to walk away from our riches if Jesus calls us to.

Most of the crowds that followed Jesus around during his earthly ministry had no idea that he would require them to sacrifice everything. To most of them, Jesus was a miracle-worker and teacher. If you wanted wisdom, healings, and free bread and fish, Jesus was your man.

But Jesus wanted to make sure they knew what he was asking from them. He would rather they not follow him at all than follow on false pretenses. So we read in the Gospel of Luke, "Now great crowds accompanied him, and he turned and said to them, 'If anyone comes to me and does not hate his own father and mother and wife and children and brothers and sisters, yes, and even his own life, he cannot be my disciple. Whoever does not bear his own cross and come after me cannot be my disciple'" (Luke 14:25–27).

Here are the plain terms of discipleship. To be a Christian, you must literally be willing to die. You must count Jesus as more important than your own parents, siblings, and children—that is what Jesus means by "hate." Let's unpack his words a little further.

First, notice *who he's talking to, his intended audience*: "If anyone would come after me." This isn't a charge just for super-Christians. He's not talking to martyrs and apostles. He's talking to everyone who wants to be a Christian. And if you would be a Christian, this must be true of you. This is the normal experience of a disciple of Jesus.

Next, consider *what you must do*. You must deny yourself. What does that mean? Well, we generally think of self-denial in terms of refraining from luxuries. If I want to lose weight, I deny myself dessert. If I want to stay within a budget, I deny myself some frivolous purchase. But Jesus means much more. Here's how John Stott describes it:

> To deny ourselves is to behave towards ourselves as Peter did towards Jesus when he denied him three times. The verb is the same (*aparneomai*). He disowned him, repudiated him, turned his back on him. Self-denial is not denying to ourselves luxuries such as chocolates, cakes, cigarettes and cocktails (although it might include this); it is actually denying or disowning ourselves, renouncing our supposed right to go our own way. "To deny oneself is . . . to turn from the idolatry of self-centeredness."[1]

Can you see why you cannot follow Jesus without denying yourself? Somebody has to call the shots in your life. It will either be you or it will be Jesus. You cannot claim to follow Jesus without denying yourself.

Then, consider *how Jesus ups the ante*. Not only must you deny yourself, but also you must take up your cross. Admittedly, we cannot quite grasp what a punch in the gut these words would have been to the disciples. We're used to crosses. We wear them as jewelry. We sing songs about them. They are everywhere. But in Jesus's day, the cross was disgusting and revolting. It was a cruel method of execution used by the Romans to keep people in the far-flung provinces from rebelling. The mere mention of a cross would probably have produced a visceral response in Jesus's hearers, much like the word "lynching" does for us today. And the disciples probably had seen people carrying their crosses. The Romans would make condemned men carry the crossbeam of the cross to the place of the execution. They knew it was a one-way trip. People carrying their cross didn't ever come back.

Now, Jesus isn't talking about dying literally (though following Jesus will require the lives of some). He's talking about dying to your old way of life. He wants us to crucify the old, self-centered way of living. It will be like death because no part of your life will go untouched.

For starters, the person who picks up his or her cross will have a different relationship with money. As Jesus says elsewhere, "Any one of you who does not renounce all that he has cannot be my disciple" (Luke 14:33). You must be dead to your possessions. They must no longer command your love and obedience. They must all be at Jesus's disposal. If he wants any of it, it's his.

Friend, anyone who told you that being a Christian requires nothing more than saying a few words or praying a prayer as if it were a magic spell, was dead wrong. Anyone who told you that coming to Jesus would make your life easy, pleasant, and fun, was dead wrong. Anyone who told you that Jesus wants you to be rich, was dead wrong. No, following Jesus means picking up your cross. As Dietrich Bonhoeffer said, "When Christ calls a man, he bids him come and die."[2]

What Kind of Treasure?

This chapter is not meant as a rant against people with money. Salvation is not a question of the balance in your checkbook. As I said earlier, it's not a sin to have money. Besides, there is no inherent virtue in being broke. Poor people can be as enslaved to their money as rich people.

Instead, this chapter means to pose the question, what love controls you? Is it a love of money? Of material possessions? Of ease and comfort and future security? Or is it a love for Jesus, the spread of his kingdom, and caring for the poor?

Every day, you store up treasure for yourself. You spend or save or invest all of your money in order to secure some kind of treasure. What kind of treasure are you buying? Jesus tells us that we must invest in him—a treasure that never fails. Everything else is a disaster, a tower that will topple over quickly. He tells us,

> Sell your possessions, and give to the needy. Provide yourselves with moneybags that do not grow old, with a treasure in the heavens that does not fail, where no thief approaches and no moth destroys. For where your treasure is, there will your heart be also. (Luke 12:33–34)

How to Respond

Reflect:

Why is money dangerous?

Why do you think Jesus told the rich young ruler to sell all that he had (Luke 18:22) when he did not tell other people to do that (cf. Luke 19:1–10)?

If you showed someone all of the ways that you use your money, what would they conclude that you value most? What does that mean about the kind of treasure you are storing up for yourself?

Can you point to areas in your life where you have "picked up your cross" and followed after Jesus? If not, what does that mean about your claim to be a Christian?

Repent:

Ask God to forgive you for the ways that you have loved and trusted your money more than him.

Think through some ways that you could use your money to serve God's purposes. Is there anything you could give up that would enable you to be more generous to the needy and the cause of the gospel?

Remember:

Read 1 Timothy 1:15: "The saying is trustworthy and deserving of full acceptance, that Christ Jesus came into the world to save sinners, of whom I am the foremost."

Jesus's death and resurrection are enough to save even the worst sinner. Thank God that he saves us, despite our greed and sin, when we come to Christ for mercy.

Report:

Show your monthly budget to someone in your church who handles their money well. Ask for a critique of your spending habits.

8

Can I Ever Really Know
If I Am a Christian?

AS WE HAVE made our way through this book, we have had to do the difficult work of taking genuinely black-and-white principles and applying them to our lives, lives which are colored in shades of gray. So the Bible is very clear about principles like these:

- You're not a Christian if you do not believe and trust in the facts of the gospel.
- You're not a Christian if you love sin.
- You're not a Christian if you do not persevere in the faith until the end.
- You're not a Christian if you don't love other people.
- You're not a Christian if you love your stuff.

But when it comes down to mapping these principles onto our lives, it gets difficult to see clearly. For example, which of these people are genuine Christians?

- Pedro is a carpenter in his early forties. He has two children and has been married to the same woman for almost twenty years. Pedro professed faith in Christ when he was a young man and has never been involved in any scandalous sin. He has been faithful in his church attendance; he's there every week. Still, Pedro has never involved himself in the life of the congregation but has kept everyone at arm's length. He does not attempt to know anyone in the congregation, or let them know him. He sits in the back of the building with a half-scowl on his face, rarely singing. He enjoys how the sermons stimulate him intellectually, but he rarely considers how to apply them to his life.

- Francisco is an international student. In his home country, Christianity is regarded as a relic from a distant past—a superstition for old ladies. Since coming to America, he has been befriended by a group of Christian students. They have included him in their outings and invited him to come along to church. Now, he finds himself wondering if he is a Christian. When he heard the news that God offers him forgiveness through Jesus, he was very excited. He finds himself resisting sin and trusting in Jesus more and more, but he still has serious doubts about whether some of the events in the Bible really happened.

- Barbara is a woman in her late twenties. She professed faith in Jesus at a youth camp when she was a teenager. In her twenties, she got married and became involved with a church in her neighborhood. But at one point, she stopped attending. Then her husband discovered that she had been having a number of affairs. He divorced her, and she became pregnant by another man, at which time she came back to the church claiming to be repentant for her sin. She got into counseling and changed her behaviors. Now she is trying to rebuild her life with her baby girl, but she is lonely and feels constantly tempted to turn to promiscuous sex for comfort.

- Alan is a teenager. His parents are Christians, and he has been in church his whole life. He prayed a prayer "to accept Jesus into his heart" and was baptized when he was a small child. He does not disbelieve in God, but he does not really see what difference Christianity makes in his life. He does not drink or do drugs or mess around with girls. But if he thought he could do those things without getting caught, he just might.

- Jenny is thirty years old. Her husband is a high-powered attorney, and she is a devoted stay-at-home mom to her three small children. She lives in the Bible Belt and attends the local Baptist church, just as all of her friends do. Though she is not (in her words) super-religious, she is glad that her children will have a religious upbringing, and it makes her feel good to give money to different church projects. She also spends a lot of time and money making sure that she and her family have the best of everything: nice clothes, a huge house, the best cars, and the most exclusive school for her children.
- Robert is a single guy in his twenties. He grew up in a Christian home and takes his faith seriously. He is involved in church, reads his Bible, and prays on his own a few times a week. He reads Christian books and listens to Christian radio. But when he goes out with his friends he sometimes drinks too much. And once or twice a week he looks at pornography on the Internet. He always feels bad about it but assumes that it's pretty much inevitable.

Which of these people are Christians? All of them, except for Francisco, profess to be Christians, and all of them could give some evidence for their faith. But they also seem to fail at least one of the tests we have outlined in this book.

If we are being really honest, who of us does not seem to fail these tests sometimes? Sometimes doubt creeps in and makes it hard to trust in Jesus. Sometimes we don't love other Christians. Sometimes sin feels enjoyable, and money looks like the answer.

Is no one a Christian? Given that we all fail to meet these standards, how could anyone claim to be a genuine follower of Christ? And how can anyone have assurance?

No Christian is perfect, but it is possible to have some confidence in one's salvation. In fact, the Bible encourages us to pursue assurance. The apostle John even wrote his first letter "to you who believe in the name of the Son of God *that you may know that you have eternal life"* (1 John 5:13). But how can weak, sinful, wavering people like us be confident that we genuinely belong to Christ? For starters, we need to identify the basis of assurance.

The Basis of Our Assurance

Every strong building must rest on a solid foundation, and the only foundation for an assurance of salvation is Jesus. Specifically, we must look to three things about Jesus: what he was like, what he has done, and what he has promised.

Christ's Character

Throughout the Gospel accounts of his life, Jesus is marked by amazing tenderness toward sinners. "And all spoke well of him," Luke says, "and marveled at the gracious words that were coming from his mouth" (Luke 4:22). The prophet Isaiah foretold that the Messiah would be tenderhearted toward the lowly—"a bruised reed he will not break, and a faintly burning wick he will not quench" (Isa. 42:3). Sometimes we view Jesus the way a wounded antelope views a lion, as if he's ready to pounce. But nothing could be further from the truth. He is not waiting for you to make a mistake so that he can condemn you. Jesus will not break us; he will not snuff us out.

In fact, Jesus's kindness toward tax collectors and prostitutes, the lowest of the low, scandalized all the "good" people (see Luke 5:30–31). You will not find one example in the Gospels of Jesus rejecting or speaking harshly to someone who was a notorious sinner. When the weak, the cripples, the unclean, the criminals, the outsiders, and the perverts came to Jesus, they always found a warm welcome and a tender word. The only people Jesus condemned were the unrepentant hypocrites, the proud, the greedy, and the self-righteous.

Jesus did not merely tolerate sinners. He came to seek and

save the lost, so he calls to them, "Come to me, all who labor and are heavy laden, and I will give you rest. Take my yoke upon you, and learn from me, *for I am gentle and lowly in heart*, and you will find rest for your souls. For my yoke is easy, and my burden is light" (Matt. 11:28–30). When we come to Jesus, we do not find him harsh and difficult to please. Instead he is gentle with the weak, and quick to pardon all of our sin and to restore us. The confidence we can have as sinners rests on the fact that Jesus is so very merciful, patient, and forbearing.

Christ's Finished Work

Our confidence can also rest on the foundation of Christ's finished work. Remember, we could never please God by even our best attempts at obedience. According to the author of Hebrews, we can have assurance before God because Jesus died, rose again, and is seated in heaven:

> Therefore, brothers, since we have confidence to enter the holy places by the blood of Jesus, by the new and living way that he opened for us through the curtain, that is, through his flesh, and since we have a great priest over the house of God, let us draw near with a true heart in full assurance of faith. (Heb. 10:19–22)

When we come to Christ, he cleanses us completely from our sin. His perfect righteousness becomes ours, even as he took all of our wickedness on himself (2 Cor. 5:21). Before, we could not approach a holy God because of our sin. Now, we can be confident that God accepts us and loves us because of what Jesus did for us.

Christ's Promises

Jesus's character and work are brought to bear through the promises that he makes to sinners, and these promises are also a foundation for our assurance. Here's a first promise from Jesus: "All that the Father gives me will come to me, and whoever comes to me I will never cast out" (John 6:37). Christians are those whom God the Father has "given" to the Son. But we should never think, "Perhaps I am not in that group of people, and so Jesus will reject me when I come to him." No, the Savior tells us that he will never cast out anyone who comes to him. We never need to fear that our sin or unloveliness will make him draw back from us.

Instead, there is a second promise for sinners like you and me: "If we confess our sins, he is faithful and just to forgive us our sins and to cleanse us from all unrighteousness" (1 John 1:9). Apart from Christ, our sin separates us from God. But Christ is faithful to forgive and cleanse us if we ask.

And if we ask, we gain a third promise: "Neither death nor life, nor angels nor rulers, nor things present nor things to come, nor powers, nor height nor depth, nor anything else in all creation, will be able to separate us from the love of God in Christ Jesus our Lord" (Rom. 8:38–39). All of God's promises of grace, mercy, and forgiveness can be ours by coming to Christ. They're his to give out (2 Cor. 1:20).

So even as we look at our own lives to see if the evidences of true faith are there, we must not imagine for a moment that our confidence can rest in what we have done. Remember the words of Jesus that we considered at the beginning of this book:

> Not everyone who says to me, "Lord, Lord," will enter the kingdom of heaven, but the one who does the will of my Father who is in heaven. On that day many will say to me, "Lord, Lord, did we not prophesy in your name, and cast out demons in your name, and do many mighty works in your name?" And then will I declare to them, "I never knew you; depart from me, you workers of lawlessness." (Matt. 7:21–23)

Notice where these deluded people placed their confidence. They were looking to their own résumé of religious accomplishments, and understandably so. They had cast out demons and prophesied and had done mighty works. So their assurance was rooted in their good deeds. But ultimately, no one will be able to compile a résumé that is able to please God and provide confidence. Instead, our only hope is that Jesus has promised salvation to anyone who repents of sin and trusts in him. On the last day, God's people will have a testimony much like the former slave trader John Newton: "My memory is nearly gone; but I remember two things: that I am a great sinner and that Christ is a great savior."[1]

We can build our assurance of salvation on no other foundation except the greatness and kindness of Christ. The great Scottish theologian John Murray put it this way:

> The faith and love of the believer have their ebb and flow. They are subject to all sorts of fluctuation, but the security of the believer rests in the faithfulness of God. . . . It is upon the determinativeness and stability of God's gifts that our hearts must rest if we are not to be driven about by the fluctuating tempers ·or temperatures of our own experience.[2]

How Can You Know?

With that firm foundation underneath us, we are ready to consider what things give believers assurance that they are truly Christians. Let me suggest four things that can give us confidence that we belong to God.

Faith in Christ Today

First, we must have faith in Christ today. The author of Hebrews wanted his readers to be certain their faith was genuine, so he writes, "For we have come to share in Christ, if indeed we hold our original confidence firm to the end" (Heb. 3:14). Later on he tells them that they can have a very certain hope in Jesus, but they must continue in faith and patience: "And we desire each one of you to show the same earnestness to have the full assurance of hope until the end, so that you may not be sluggish, but imitators of those who through faith and patience inherit the promises" (Heb. 6:11–12). We inherit the promises through patiently holding onto our faith.

Paul said something similar to the Colossians. He said they could have great confidence in their salvation if they "continue in the faith, stable and steadfast, not shifting from the hope of the gospel" (Col. 1:23). As we saw back in chapter 5, a genuine Christian will endure in the faith. Thus, the important question is not, "Have I professed faith in Christ in the past?" but rather, "Am I trusting Christ right now for my salvation?" If you must point back to some distant event for evidence that you have an interest in Christ, you might wonder if you are genuinely saved. But if you have continued trusting Christ over time, you have reason to have hope in your salvation.

Do you struggle with doubting yourself? Then stop thinking about yourself this very second, turn the eyes of your heart toward him, and trust him. Do it right now!

The Presence of God's Spirit

The indwelling presence of the Holy Spirit in our lives is another firm indication that we are a child of God. Christians have the Holy Spirit dwelling in them; non-Christians do not. Notice all the "if" statements Paul uses in this passage:

> You, however, are not in the flesh but in the Spirit, *if* in fact the Spirit of God dwells in you. Anyone who does not have the Spirit of Christ does not belong to him. But *if* Christ is in you, although the body is dead because of sin, the Spirit is life because of righteousness. *If* the Spirit of him who raised Jesus from the dead dwells in you, he who raised Christ Jesus from

the dead will also give life to your mortal bodies through his Spirit who dwells in you. (Rom. 8:9–11)

How then do we know that the Spirit of God is present in our lives? In one sense it can be difficult to know. Being indwelt by the Spirit is not the same as getting a tattoo, which leaves an obvious physical mark. But there are a several helpful indicators:

- *We believe correct doctrine about God.* We can only believe rightly through the Spirit. Paul observes that "no one can say 'Jesus is Lord' except in the Holy Spirit" (1 Cor. 12:3). John also says that if "we believe in the name of his Son Jesus Christ," then "we know that he abides in us, by the Spirit whom he has given us" (1 John 3:23–24).
- *The Spirit bears the fruit in our lives.* You can tell where the Spirit is at work because his fingerprints will be on a believer's life. "The fruit of the Spirit is love, joy, peace, patience, kindness, goodness, faithfulness, gentleness, self-control. . . . And those who belong to Christ Jesus have crucified the flesh with its passions and desires" (Gal. 5:22–24).
- *God's Spirit also testifies to us that we are children of God.* A believer will normally have a subjective inner sense that they are being led by God's Spirit to follow him and cry out to him as our Father. So Paul writes, "And because you are sons, God has sent the Spirit of his Son into our hearts, crying, 'Abba! Father!'" (Gal. 4:6). Elsewhere, he wrote, "For all who are led by the Spirit of God are sons of God. For you did not receive the spirit of slavery to fall back into fear, but you have received the Spirit of adoption as sons, by whom we cry, 'Abba! Father!' The Spirit himself bears witness with our spirit that we are children of God" (Rom. 8:14–16).

Obedience to the Word of God

A third matter for giving us confidence in our salvation is our obedience to the Word of God. As we saw in chapter 4, the presence of unchecked sin in our lives should provoke us to consider whether we are really Christians. In contrast, the presence of the Holy Spirit's fruit (above) should encourage us that we belong to God. If we love Jesus, we will keep his commandments (John 14:15). Like David, we will be able to say that God's Word is not a burden but is sweet like honey (Ps. 19:10).

Again, it's important to remember that we shouldn't imagine that we will ever perfectly keep God's law or exhibit the fruit of the Spirit in this world. Rather, it's a question of the trajectory of our lives. Would the people who know you well say that you are generally characterized by obedience to God?

You should examine your day-in, day-out attitude toward the Word of God. Do you generally see the wisdom of God's law? Do you delight to obey him? Even now, what is your attitude toward this very exercise? The Bible tells us to examine ourselves and make our calling sure. Do you do that, or do you take your salvation for granted?

A Pattern of Growth over Time

Fourth and finally, a believer should look for a pattern of growth in spiritual maturity over time. The genuineness of our faith is marked out less by our current spiritual maturity and more by the overall pattern of our lives. At any one moment you may feel bogged down in sin, weary, and struggling to grow. Perhaps you have been losing your temper with your kids lately, or you've had a disrespectful attitude toward your boss. You know it is wrong, but it seems like you cannot get a grip in this area of your life. Does that mean that you are not a Christian?

Not necessarily. To get a good read on your spiritual condition, look at the big picture. Have you seen any growth in your life in these areas? Even if you are disappointed in yourself right now, can you see ways in which you have changed and matured in the past five years?

I once heard a very helpful illustration of what the Christian life should look like from counseling professor David Powlison. He said the pattern of Christian life and growth is like a yo-yo: up and down, up and down. That is pretty depressing, but also pretty true. One day I feel as if I have sin beat; the next day I feel as if I am back at the beginning.

But there is more, Powlison said. The pattern of Christian life and growth may be like a yo-yo, but it's a yo-yo in the hands of someone walking up a flight of stairs. That is a much more encouraging image. In the day-to-day, we are acutely aware of the yo-yo feeling, the ups and downs of the battle against sin. But we miss the larger picture of growth and maturity that God is graciously working in us—he is carrying us up the stairs. Even our low points now are higher than our high points used to be.[3]

So you might still struggle with bursts of anger at your children (up and down, up and down). But if you are a Christian, over time you (and your friends) will see that you are gradually becoming more loving, that your outbursts of anger are rarer, less violent, shorter in duration, and that you are quicker to repent and seek reconciliation.

What If I Am Not a Christian?

John Wesley was an Anglican minister and the son of an Anglican minister. By 1738, he was well known in England for his piety and his strict and methodical approach to his religion. He was not, however, a Christian. By his own admission he was trusting in his own goodness to earn God's favor. He thought that his religious performance would make him right with God.

Then one day in May, right after Wesley had returned from a failed missions trip to the Americas, he had an experience of understanding God's grace. He wrote in his journal,

> In the evening I went very unwillingly to a society [meeting] in Aldersgate Street, where one was reading Luther's preface to the *Epistle of the Romans*. About a quarter before nine, while [the leader] was describing the change which God works in the heart through faith in Christ, I felt my heart strangely warmed. I felt I did trust in Christ, Christ alone, for my salvation; and an assurance was given me that He had taken away *my* sins, even *mine*, and saved *me* from the law of sin and death.[4]

I hope you have known that same warming of heart, the same assurance that Christ has taken away your sins.

It is my prayer that this book has had one of two effects on you, depending on where you are with God:

- If you are a genuine Christian, I hope that this book has been a helpful exercise for you in heeding the Bible's call to examine yourself and make your calling and election sure. I pray that you are more confident of God's love for you and more amazed at the way he has changed you and shaped you by his marvelous salvation.
- If you are a nominal Christian—a Christian in name only, as John Wesley was—I hope this book has been used of God to open your eyes to your spiritual danger. I pray that the Lord would show you that, despite what you have said and thought, you are still in need of his salvation.

Friend, if you are not a Christian, you must not delay. Turn from your sins and put your trust in Jesus. You will find him ready to save you.

How to Respond

Reflect:

> Look back at the examples at the beginning of the chapter. What basis for assurance do those people have? What in their lives is concerning?

How can imperfect people ever really know if they are saved?

Why must our confidence in our salvation be rooted in Jesus's character, work, and promises? What happens if we only look at our own deeds and attitudes for assurance?

Why is it important for genuine believers to have assurance that they are God's children? How would they relate to God differently if they were not sure that they were saved?

Are you a Christian?

Repent:

Confess to God the ways that you have trusted in your own works for your salvation and taken credit for God's grace in your life.

If you see evidence of God's saving grace in your life, take time to praise him and give him glory for them.

Remember:

Read Colossians 2:13–14: "And you, who were dead in your trespasses and the uncircumcision of your flesh, God made alive together with him, having forgiven us all our trespasses, by canceling the record of debt that stood against us with its legal demands. This he set aside, nailing it to the cross."

The work of Christ means that we who were once dead in our sins are now alive. Jesus took all of our sin and guilt and nailed it to the cross. There is nothing we need to do in order to earn that forgiveness; it is a free gift of God to all who trust in Jesus for it.

Report:

Ask someone in your church to evaluate your life according to the criteria laid out in this book. Solicit feedback about your spiritual health.

9

A Little Help from
Your Friends

MY PLANE ARRIVED at London's Heathrow Airport at about 6:00 a.m. I had only traveled internationally a few times, so the rigors of the transatlantic red-eye had taken the spring out of my step. My mouth was dry and my face was gray. A trip to an airport coffee shop went badly when they would not sell me a normal, regular drip coffee but could only offer a café Americano.

Finally, I made my way through baggage claim and was met by a cab driver named Chas. Chas, who was very well dressed, had been sent by the missions group for whom I was speaking that week. He was old enough to be my grandfather but, strangely enough, he kept calling me "sir." After a while I asked him to call me Mike, since, as an American, I was uncomfortable with formality and anything that smacked of class distinction. Chas explained that as an Englishman he was uncomfortable with anything that smacked of familiarity. But he agreed to call me Mike, since I was the customer and got to call the shots.

As soon as we were underway, Chas began to tell me how he became a Christian. He had been addicted to drugs and alcohol until a woman told him the good news about Jesus and he was immediately born again. We had a pleasant conversation during the car ride, but by the time we neared the city of Luton (think Cleveland without whatever it is that might make Cleveland inhabitable), I was struggling to keep the conversation going. Searching for topics, I asked Chas about the church he attended.

Suddenly, the tenor of the conversation changed. Chas dropped the polite English façade and gripped the wheel tightly. "I don't go to church," he told me. "I have everything I need here in my car. I listen to sermons on the radio, and I have fellowship with the people that I drive, people like you. I do not need to be part of a church in order to be a Christian."

Well, what do you think of Chas's argument? Do you need to be a member of a local church in order to be a Christian? Or is it purely optional?

On one hand Chas was correct. It's theoretically possible to be a genuine Christian without being part of a church. It's also theoretically possible for two people to be married without ever living in the same house. But that doesn't mean it's a good idea, or even possible in any meaningful sense. A Christian who is not part of a local church is not living the way Jesus intended his people to live. Among other things, you're going to have an especially hard time knowing if you really are a Christian. With this final chapter, let's look and see how membership and involvement in a local church are important parts of God's plan to help us know whether we are Christians.

Church Membership and Assurance

As you look at what Scripture says, you see that the church has been given a few jobs to do. For example, the church is called to preach the gospel to all nations (Matt. 28:19–20; Acts 1:8). The church is also Jesus's appointed means for making it clear both to the world and to itself who is a Christian and who isn't.

As we considered at the beginning of this book, many

people are confused about their spiritual state. Many are genu-ine believers, but they struggle with fearing they are not. More frighteningly, many sincerely believe they are Christians, but they are sincerely wrong. Meanwhile, the world looks at the church and, with this latter category especially, sees no real difference between professing believers and the world.

But if local churches were doing their job, it would not be so—and books like this one might not be necessary. This is where church membership comes in. Churches should be made up of people who are genuinely converted. In that sense, one function of church membership is to give assurance of salvation. Being a church member means the church believes that your profession of faith is credible. That's why the church has baptized you, gives you the Lord's Supper, and has not disciplined you. Another function of church membership is to show the world what it means to be a true Christian, since it excludes unbelievers and false professors from membership.

Obviously, no human being or church can see into the soul and determine the eternal destiny of another person. And we should not assume that any particular church is perfectly pure. Still, churches have been given a representative authority by Jesus to speak on his behalf, weigh the credibility of people's professions of faith, and establish new communities of believ-ers around the world. However imperfectly churches exercise that authority, it remains their divinely mandated right and responsibility.[1]

So let's take the example of my cabbie friend Chas. He heard the gospel and responded in genuine repentance and faith—from what I could discern in a 45-minute car ride. Now, he represents Jesus to the world around him. Everyone who climbs into his cab hears about Jesus, and rightly so.

But what if Chas is wrong? What if his profession of faith is not genuine and Chas is self-deceived? What if there is unrepentant sin in his life to the extent that it calls his conversion into question? For the sake of illustration, let's say that over time Chas began to change. He started to rip off customers, swear loudly at other drivers in traffic, and make advances toward female passengers. But he keeps calling himself a Christian. Now we have two significant problems: On the one hand a man may be deluded into thinking he is converted. On the other hand he is lying to the people around him about what Jesus and Jesus's people are like. That is one of the problems that membership in the local church is supposed to address. This is done in three ways.

Baptism

In the Bible, baptism is the normal and prescribed way for a believer to manifest his or her faith publicly and join the membership of the church. Baptism is a two-sided coin. On one side, the believer self-identifies as a Christian. On the other, the church affirms the credibility of that profession and administers the sign and seal of baptism.

So if a notorious atheist came to a church asking to be baptized, that church would want to carefully examine his life and ask probing questions before agreeing to baptize him. Anything less would reduce baptism to a meaningless splash in a pool.

The Lord's Supper

If baptism is the initiatory rite for the Christian, the Lord's Supper is how the believer expresses ongoing faith in Christ and connection to the church body. Like baptism, there are two sides to the Lord Supper. The believer comes to the table because he or she identifies as a Christian. The church admits the individual to the table because his or her life and conduct seems consistent with true Christian faith.

Corrective Discipline

Baptism and admittance to the Lord's Supper are meant to help assure believers that their profession of faith is genuine. If over time, however, the course of a person's life and conduct begins to indicate a lack of salvation, then the church is obligated to step in and make that clear.

The apostle Paul faced a situation like this at the church in Corinth. A man who was part of the church was engaging in scandalous sin, and the church actually affirmed his behavior instead of confronting it. So Paul wrote to the church to correct their error.

> It is actually reported that there is sexual immorality among you, and of a kind that is not tolerated even among pagans, for a man has his father's wife. And you are arrogant! Ought you not rather to mourn? Let him who has done this be removed from among you.
>
> For though absent in body, I am present in spirit; and as if present, I have already pronounced judgment on the one who did such a thing. When you are assembled in the name of the Lord Jesus and my spirit is present, with the power of our Lord Jesus, you are to deliver this man to Satan for the destruction of the flesh, so that his spirit may be saved in the day of the Lord. (1 Cor. 5:1–5)

Paul tells the church to remove this man from the membership of the congregation, an action made visible by refusing to admit him to the Lord's Supper. He concludes, "But now I am writing to you not to associate with anyone who bears the name of brother if he is guilty of sexual immorality or greed, or is an idolater, reviler, drunkard, or swindler—not even to eat with such a one" (1 Cor. 5:11).

The purpose of this discipline is twofold. First, Paul wanted the straying brother to be restored—so that his spirit may be saved. Putting the man out of the church was a way of saying to him, "The way you are living does not match with your profession, so our church can no longer affirm your profession." The hope was that such an action and such words would lead such a man to repent and turn to Christ for forgiveness.

Second, the church's action said something to the world around it. This man's relationship was so repulsive that even the pagans would be scandalized by it. So the church's disciplinary action would help these pagans see that someone living in flagrant and unrepentant sin was not a Christian.

Thus Jesus authorized the church to help publicly establish who is a Christian and who is not. By baptizing believers, celebrating the Lord's Supper, and exercising corrective discipline, the church puts a stamp of approval on a believer's profession of faith. It's a hedge against self-deception.

So if you want help knowing whether you are a Christian, find a local church that believes and teaches the Bible. Ask them to help you examine yourself. Then if you conclude together that you are a believer, ask to be baptized and joined to the church's membership.

The Arena for Our Faith

If you remember, we saw at the outset of this book that five things always characterize genuine faith in Christ:

> *Belief in true doctrine.* You're not a Christian just because you like Jesus.
> *Hatred for sin in your life.* You're not a Christian if you enjoy sin.
> *Perseverance over time.* You're not a Christian if you don't persist in the faith.
> *Love for other people.* You're not a Christian if you don't have care and concern for other people.
> *Freedom from love of the world.* You're not a Christian if the things of the world are more valuable to you than God.

Just as a church should remove people who appear to be false professors, so it should build up those who appear to be true professors.[2] Let's turn now and consider how participating in a local church will help you live out some of the things discussed in this book.

Belief in True Doctrine

The church is called to preach true doctrine, specifically the contents of God's Word whose message centers on the message of Christ's life, death, and resurrection. So Paul writes to Timothy, a pastor in the church at Ephesus, and commands him to teach nothing but the truth of God's Word:

> Preach the word; be ready in season and out of season; reprove, rebuke, and exhort, with complete patience and teaching. For the time is coming when people will not endure sound teaching, but having itching ears they will accumulate for themselves teachers to suit their own passions, and will turn away from listening to the truth and wander off into myths. As for you, always be sober-minded, endure suffering, do the work of an evangelist, fulfill your ministry. (2 Tim. 4:2–5)

Along the same lines, Jesus gives leaders to his churches, so that those leaders will instruct the congregation in the truth. Paul writes elsewhere,

> And [Jesus] gave the apostles, the prophets, the evangelists, the shepherds and teachers, to equip the saints for the work of ministry, for building up the body of Christ, until we all attain to the unity of the faith and of the knowledge of the Son of God, to mature manhood, to the measure of the stature of the fullness of Christ, so that we may no longer be children, tossed to and fro by the waves and carried about by every wind of doctrine, by human cunning, by craftiness in deceitful schemes. (Eph. 4:11–14)

The risen Christ has equipped the church so that it will not be deceived by false doctrine. Teachers teach the truth and elders protect the church from "wolves" (Acts 20:29–31).

So membership in a healthy congregation will bring you into regular contact with the proclamation of God's truth. As you hear the Word of God with other believers, you will be strengthened in your faith and inoculated against error. And putting yourself under the care of godly leaders will protect you from those who would deceive you and lead you astray. In a world that is skeptical and cynical, it's helpful, no, necessary, to have regular contact with like-minded believers, even if only to be reminded that you are not crazy for believing this stuff.

Hatred for Sin in Your Life

Membership in a church should also help you to grow in hating sin. As the Word is preached, you will understand more clearly what sin is, how badly sin lies, and how Christians have better promises to rest in. The world around us does not value the Bible's teaching on these matters. Television peddles the virtues of lust and disrespect. Advertising encourages greed and envy. The Old Country Buffet down the street stays in business by fomenting gluttony. But in the church you have a place where godliness is valued, expected, and promulgated.

Brothers and sisters in the church must admonish each other (Col. 3:16), teach and train each other regarding what's appropriate (Titus 2:3–4), and urge self-control (Titus 2:6). So the author of Hebrews tells Christians to continue meeting together to encourage each other toward godliness: "And let us consider how to stir up one another to love and good works, not neglecting to meet together, as is the habit of some, but encouraging one another, and all the more as you see the Day drawing near" (Heb. 10:24–25).

In addition, being involved in a church will provide you

with an arena in which you will have opportunities to say no to sin. In Galatians 5, Paul lists a whole host of sins that believers are told to reject: "Now the works of the flesh are evident: sexual immorality, impurity, sensuality, idolatry, sorcery, *enmity, strife, jealousy, fits of anger, rivalries, dissensions, divisions, envy,* drunkenness, orgies, and things like these. I warn you, as I warned you before, that those who do such things will not inherit the kingdom of God" (Gal. 5:19–21). Did you notice that string of sins right there in the middle? They are the kinds of sins that emerge in a community. Isolated individuals don't normally need to concern themselves about jealousy, enmity, or strife because no one's around to make them jealous or angry. But life in a church filled with sinners like you will give you plenty of opportunities both to experience these temptations and to fight against them.

There are many sins you will never have the opportunity to put off if your "fellowship" is restricted to what you experience in a taxicab. Chas the cabbie seemed like a good guy; he was friendly and patient. But let's be honest, he didn't have to spend much time in my presence. He never got to know what I am like when I am stressed or irritable. He never had to be patient with my sin or forbearing with my selfishness. Not only was he missing an opportunity to know himself truly, he was missing the opportunity to know other believers like me and help them with their sin. Life in the church helps us hate sin, and it helps us help others to hate sin.

Perseverance in the Faith

Do you remember when I pointed out in chapter 5 how Jesus said that "the one who endures to the end will be saved" (Matt. 10:22)? Church membership helps us to do that—to persevere in the faith to the end.

In Hebrews 3, we are instructed to:

> Take care, brothers, lest there be in any of you an evil, un-
> believing heart, leading you to fall away from the living God.
> But exhort one another every day, as long as it is called "today,"
> that none of you may be hardened by the deceitfulness of sin.
> For we have come to share in Christ, if indeed we hold our orig-
> inal confidence firm to the end. (Heb. 3:12–14)

The writer tells us to exhort one another so that we will not become hardened by the deceitfulness of sin. Again, how can the lone Christian do that and not become hardened and self-deceived? In the church, we form relationships with brothers and sisters who get to know us, who commit to doing good in our lives, and who then exhort us every day to remain faithful. When they see us wandering away, they try to restore us to the faith (James 5:19-20).

Love for Others

If you remember, we saw that Christians are to be characterized by love for their enemies, love for the needy, and love for other Christians. In a sense, membership in a local church gives us a chance to do all three. As D. A. Carson has pointed out in his book *Love in Hard Places*, loving another Christian is loving someone who used to be an enemy, an enemy of God and of all humanity, just as you once were. Now, in the church, these enemies learn to love one another practically and concretely.

In the church, too, we learn to love those who are needy, needy both physically and spiritually. The world tends to push off those who are needy. But a church should embrace them.

I don't want to restrict our love for our enemies, the needy, or other Christians to our own local church, but it's the best place to begin. Can you love your Christian friend who goes to a different church? Of course. In fact, you should. But it's in the context of the local church that our most important interactions with other Christians take place, since these are the people who have covenanted to oversee our discipleship, and we theirs.

Paul describes in Ephesians what love in the local church should look like:

> I therefore, a prisoner for the Lord, urge you to walk in a manner worthy of the calling to which you have been called, with all humility and gentleness, with patience, bearing with one another in love, eager to maintain the unity of the Spirit in the bond of peace. There is one body and one Spirit—just as you were called to the one hope that belongs to your call—one Lord, one faith, one baptism, one God and Father of all, who is over all and through all and in all. (Eph. 4:1–6)

Walking in a manner worthy of our calling means showing patience, bearing with others in love, and maintaining unity. That normally happens in the local church, an actual assembly of the body of Christ.

In fact, I think this is one of the main reasons that so many professing Christians either do not attend church or avoid committing to one particular congregation. Being in a church requires love. It requires selflessness. It requires us to put the interests of others ahead of our own (Phil. 2:3–4). They simply do not want to be inconvenienced by having to love other Christians.

After all, let's face it: love is costly and Christians are messy. If you plug into a local church, they will probably put you to work. You will be asked to serve other Christians (maybe even by watching their kids in the nursery!), and you will find yourself surrounded by some broken, weak, needy people. That might sound like a bad deal at first. But if you remember the love and service of Christ for you (Mark 10:43–45), and if you realize that you probably require more love and patience than you realize, you will find yourself blessed in the church.

Materialism

The church is a society of people who have a greater treasure than anything in this world. Members of the church pool their money together to support the ministry of the congregation, help with the relief of the poor, and spread the gospel around the world. Out in the world, wealth makes you important. Not so in the church. So James tells his readers that God has a different kind of economy:

> My brothers, show no partiality as you hold the faith in our Lord Jesus Christ, the Lord of glory. For if a man wearing a gold ring and fine clothing comes into your assembly, and a poor man in shabby clothing also comes in, and if you pay attention to the one who wears the fine clothing and say, "You sit here in a good place," while you say to the poor man, "You stand over there," or, "Sit down at my feet," have you not then made distinctions among yourselves and become judges with evil thoughts? Listen, my beloved brothers, has not God chosen those who are poor in the world to be rich in faith and heirs of the kingdom, which he has promised to those who love him? (James 2:1–5)

Finally . . .

Now, I realize that all of what I have described above is the ideal. No church will perfectly encourage you and embody the principles of the Bible. But just because the church is not perfect yet does not mean that you should head off on your own. Instead, you should enlist the help of people in your local church as you examine your life. As you seek to make your calling and election sure, do so in the context of a community of loving and discerning Christians.

Toward the end of his final letter, with his death looming on the horizon, the apostle Paul wrote,

> For I am already being poured out as a drink offering, and the time of my departure has come. I have fought the good fight, I have finished the race, I have kept the faith. Henceforth there is

laid up for me the crown of righteousness, which the Lord, the righteous judge, will award to me on that Day, and not only to me but also to all who have loved his appearing. (2 Tim. 4:6–8)

My prayer is that when you come to the end of your life, you will be able to say the same thing.

How to Respond

Reflect:

How would you answer Chas's assertion that he does not need to be involved in a church?

Does it matter if you are committed to one particular church, or is it enough to hop from church to church each Sunday?

How does living in community with other people give us opportunities to say no to some specific sins? What good fruit of the Spirit can we only show in the presence of other people?

Repent:

Confess to God any individualism or distaste for authority that has kept you from being involved in a local church.

Make a plan for finding a church to which you can commit.

Remember:

Ephesians 5:25–27 reads, ". . . Christ loved the church and gave himself up for her, that he might sanctify her, having cleansed her by the washing of water with the word, so that he might present the church to himself in splendor, without spot or wrinkle or any such thing, that she might be holy and without blemish."

We were not holy and without blemish when Christ died for us. Instead, he died for sinners. Praise him that anyone who comes to him finds him ready to cleanse and forgive!

Report:

Talk to the leadership of your church about becoming a member so that you can be fully accountable.

Ask someone in the church to commit to helping you for one year so that you can grow in each of the areas mentioned in this chapter.

Acknowledgments

I OWE A FEW PEOPLE a lot of thanks for their help with this book.

First, this book was the idea of my friend Andrew Sherwood. I think it was a good idea, even if his far more obnoxious title ultimately got the ax.

Second, Jonathan Leeman is a great editor. It is fun to work with a good friend who "gets" the project and laughs at your lame jokes.

Third, I am grateful to the good people at Crossway for their support for this project. I am very thankful to be working with such a classy outfit.

Fourth, the good people of Guilford Baptist Church have been a marvelous encouragement to me. I can't imagine any church that makes it more of a joy for their pastor to serve them. Special thanks are due to Brian and Leslie Roe for their friendship and hospitality during the writing process.

Finally, my family. My children Kendall, Knox, Phineas, and Ebenezer have been so sweet and patient while my attention has been devoted to this book. And my wife, Karen, is undoubtedly the most encouraging, self-sacrificing, supportive, and patient woman on the planet. Being married to her is a daily reminder that God loves me far more than I deserve.

Notes

Chapter One: *You Are Not a Christian Just Because You Say That You Are*

1. Roald Dahl, *Willy Wonka & the Chocolate Factory,* directed by Mel Stuart (Burbank, CA: Warner Home Video, 1971), DVD.

Chapter Three: *You Are Not a Christian Just Because You Like Jesus*

1. James Beverly, "Comment: Buddhism's guru, part two," canadian christianity.com, accessed August 11, 2010, http://www.canadianchristianity.com/cgi-bin/na.cgi?nationalupdates/040415comment.

2. Sankar Ghose, *Mahatma Gandhi* (New Delhi: Allied, 1991), 37.

3. Quoted in John Farrell, *The Day Without Yesterday: Lemaître, Einstein, and the Birth of Modern Cosmology* (New York: Avalon, 2005), 202.

4. Quoted in Thomas Schreiner, *New Testament Theology: Magnifying God in Christ* (Grand Rapids, MI: Baker, 2008), 331n94.

5. E.g., Rom. 11:26; 1 Cor. 1:31; 2 Cor. 3:16.

6. Leon Morris, *The Cross in the New Testament* (Grand Rapids, MI: Eerdmans, 1965), 410.

7. Sam Allberry, *Lifted: Experiencing the Resurrection Life* (Nottingham: Inter-Varsity Press, 2010), 20.

8. Michael Wittmer, *Don't Stop Believing: Why Living Like Jesus Is Not Enough,* Kindle edition (Grand Rapids, MI: Zondervan, 2008), 44.

Chapter Four: *You Are Not a Christian If You Enjoy Sin*

1. This is not to say that unbelievers are completely wicked and that apart from Christ we would do nothing but evil things all the time. Instead, our plight before Christ is that sin (e.g., selfishness, pride, greed) is a driving and controlling force. It cannot be resisted; it is the operating principle of human life apart from Christ.

2. Schreiner, *New Testament Theology,* 551.

3. If you count that quick trip to Taco Bell I just took, you should probably add gluttony to the list.

4. Colin Kruse, *The Letters of John* (Grand Rapids, MI: Eerdmans, 2000), 70.

5. The story continues on and tells us about what happens to the older brother, but it's not applicable to our purposes here. If you want to know how the story ends, read Luke 15:11–32.

Chapter Five: *You Are Not a Christian If You Do Not Endure to the End*

1. After reading from several of these sites, it is amazing how they all beat themselves up and express regret for having had such certainty about their faith in Christ. But now they have the same amount of certainty about their lack of faith! You would think they would have gained at least some intellectual humility in the process.

2. John Hammett, *Biblical Foundations for Baptist Churches: A Contemporary Ecclesiology* (Grand Rapids, MI: Kregel, 2005), 109.

3. Kruse, *The Letters of John*, 2.

4. The New Hampshire Baptist Confession (1833), article XI.

Chapter Six: You Are Not a Christian If You Don't Love Other People

1. Charles Dickens, *A Christmas Carol* (New York: Bantam, 1986), 2.

2. Ibid., 85.

3. I was thinking of Thanksgiving, our national declaration of our love for football and roasted meat. Upon reading this portion of the manuscript, my wife pointed out that some people might more naturally think of Valentine's Day. Either way is fine with me.

4. E.g., 1 Pet. 2:17; Rom. 12:10; 2 John 5.

5. Quoted in Martin Hengel, *Poverty and Riches in the Early Church: Aspects of a Social History of Early Christianity* (Minneapolis, MN: Fortress, 1998), 67–68.

Chapter Seven: You Are Not a Christian If You Love Your Stuff

1. John R. W. Stott, *The Cross of Christ* (Nottingham: Inter-Varsity, 1986), 279.

2. Dietrich Bonhoeffer, *The Cost of Discipleship* (New York: Simon and Schuster, 1995), 89.

Chapter Eight: Can I Ever Really Know If I Am a Christian?

1. Quoted in Jerry Bridges, *Respectable Sins: Confronting the Sins We Tolerate* (Colorado Springs, CO: NavPress, 2007), 31.

2. John Murray, *The Collected Writings of John Murray, vol. 2, Lectures in Systematic Theology* (Carlisle: Banner of Truth, 1977), 270–71.

3. Paul David Tripp and David Powlison, *Changing Hearts, Changing Lives*, session 2 (Greensboro, NC: New Growth, 2006), DVD.

4. Quoted in Mark Noll, *Turning Points: Decisive Moments in the History of Christianity* (Grand Rapids, MI: Baker, 1997), 225–26.

Chapter Nine: A Little Help from Your Friends

1. If you want a good and careful defense of this concept, see Jonathan Leeman, *The Church and the Surprising Offense of God's Love: Reintroducing the Doctrines of Church Membership and Discipline* (Wheaton, IL: Crossway, 2010), 182–217.

2. Theologians call the former "corrective discipline" and the latter "formative discipline."

General Index

Scripture Index